The Somme
24 June –19 November 1916

Richard Doherty

NORTHERN IRELAND
WAR MEMORIAL

ACCREDITED
MUSEUM

NORTHERN IRELAND WAR MEMORIAL

Published in 2016 by
Northern Ireland War Memorial
21 Talbot Street Belfast BT1 2LD
www.niwarmemorial.org
ISBN 978-0-9929301-7-2

The rights of Richard Doherty
as author of this book have
been asserted in accordance
with the Copyright, Design
and Patents Act 1988.

Design, maps, Illustrations
by John McMillan

Printed by
GPS Colour Graphics Ltd

Acknowledgements

Although the author's name is usually the only one to appear on the cover and title page of a book, there will always be many others involved in the book's evolution. This is especially so with books on military history and this work is no exception. When I was asked to write this volume to mark the centenary of the Somme campaign and the role played in that campaign by Irishmen I knew that I could rely on a wide range of experts and institutions to assist my work. To all of them I offer grateful thanks for their assistance.

The institutions that helped include the National Archives, Kew, Richmond, Surrey, where the war diaries of the formations and units involved in the campaign are held. I have been researching there for over thirty years and am always impressed by the professionalism and helpfulness of the staff. Today researching at Kew is simpler, but less personal, since most of the war diaries of the First World War, the Great War to those who lived through it, are digitised and may be downloaded at home by a researcher. The Imperial War Museum, London, is another indispensable archive and its collection of photographs is especially useful. Many IWM photographs appear in this book and I thank the Museum for its co-operation. Libraries NI, especially Belfast and Derry Central Libraries, were also valuable sources of information and assisted in locating books that were long out of print. The Linen Hall Library in Belfast did likewise. The support of enthusiastic and professional librarians has long been a great asset to many historians.

Special thanks are due to the Very Reverend Doctor William Morton, Dean of Derry and Rector of Templemore, for access to the archives of St Columb's Cathedral, and to Ian Bartlett of the Cathedral for his help in tracking down photographs and providing information, especially on the Hamilton Band. Thanks also to the Presbyterian Historical Society, specifically Valerie Adams, Ann Robinson and Colin Walker, for providing a photograph of the Reverend James Gilbert Paton.

My good friend David Truesdale, in spite of being embroiled in the production of a new history of 36th (Ulster) Division, was generous with his time and support and with information that assisted me in the writing of this book. Gardiner Mitchell, author of *Three Cheers for the Derrys!*, the outstanding history of 10th (Derry Service) Battalion Royal Inniskilling Fusiliers, also provided invaluable support as well as several photographs that appear in the book. Colonel Hubert and Mrs Sandra McAllister permitted the photographing of the Bible and bullet belonging to Sandra's Grandfather, Private William Cordner of 9th Princess Victoria's (Royal Irish Fusiliers), thus helping to bring to life a remarkable story of survival in the horror of the advance of 9th Faughs on 1 July 1916.

To Derek Smyth and Ian Montgomery are due thanks for their diligent reading and checking of the text while Professor John McMillan has done an excellent job in designing and laying out the book. Tim Webster allowed several of his excellent maps of the Somme campaign to be adapted for the book for which I thank him.

I also wish to express my gratitude to my fellow trustees of the Northern Ireland War Memorial for commissioning me to write this book and to the staff of the NIWM for their support, especially to Ciaran Elizabeth Doran, formerly Curator/Manager, Jenny Haslett, Museum Manager, Kerry McIvor, Collections and Communications Co-ordinator, and Victoria Gibson, Finance Manager. My wife, Carol, my children, Joanne, James and Catríona, my son in law, Steven, and grandchildren Cíaran, Katrina, Joshua and Sophie, give me their constant support, without which I could not devote time to research and writing.

Finally, any errors in the book are my own and not the fault of any of those who have assisted me with the research and writing.

Richard Doherty
Prehen May 2016

Foreword

It is often said that history is lived forwards, but understood backwards. These words spoken in the spring of 1916 by Lieutenant General Sir Henry Rawlinson took on a poignant note as his Fourth Army was moved from the plains of Flanders to open a new offensive on the River Somme:

> it is capital country in which to undertake an offensive when we get sufficiency of artillery, for the observation is excellent, and with plenty of guns and ammunition we ought to be able to avoid the heavy losses which the infantry have always suffered on previous occasions.

But the same rolling chalk landscape, so much more like the south of England for the British, provided the Germans with suitable ground for defence, being able to construct deep dugouts in the chalk resistant to most artillery shells.

The resultant colossal casualties and significant gains of the first day are forever recalled in the annals of the British Army. The very words 'The Somme' seem to toll like an especially ominous bell in Ulster even today. But as Richard Doherty explains in this scrupulously researched book, soldiers from all over Ireland distinguished themselves in the battles of the Somme campaign.

One of the aims of the Northern Ireland War Memorial Museum is to commemorate these times and these combatants. Richard Doherty succeeds admirably in guiding the reader through the complexities of this sustained and epic campaign.

Ian Wilson
Chairman, Northern Ireland War Memorial

CONTENTS

1916   CALENDAR   1916

	Sun.	Mon.	Tues.	Wed.	Thur.	Fri.	Sat.		Sun.	Mon.	Tues.	Wed.	Thur.	Fri.	Sat.
Jan.							1	**July**							1
	2	3	4	5	6	7	8		2	3	4	5	6	7	8
	9	10	11	12	13	14	15		9	10	11	12	13	14	15
	16	17	18	19	20	21	22		16	17	18	19	20	21	22
	23	24	25	26	27	28	29		23	24	25	26	27	28	29
	30	31							30	31					
Feb.			1	2	3	4	5	**Aug.**			1	2	3	4	5
	6	7	8	9	10	11	12		6	7	8	9	10	11	12
	13	14	15	16	17	18	19		13	14	15	16	17	18	19
	20	21	22	23	24	25	26		20	21	22	23	24	25	26
	27	28	29						27	28	29	30	31		
Mar.				1	2	3	4	**Sept.**						1	2
	5	6	7	8	9	10	11		3	4	5	6	7	8	9
	12	13	14	15	16	17	18		10	11	12	13	14	15	16
	19	20	21	22	23	24	25		17	18	19	20	21	22	23
	26	27	28	29	30	31			24	25	26	27	28	29	30
April							1	**Oct.**	1	2	3	4	5	6	7
	2	3	4	5	6	7	8		8	9	10	11	12	13	14
	9	10	11	12	13	14	15		15	16	17	18	19	20	21
	16	17	18	19	20	21	22		22	23	24	25	26	27	28
	23	24	25	26	27	28	29		29	30	31				
	30														
May		1	2	3	4	5	6	**Nov.**				1	2	3	4
	7	8	9	10	11	12	13		5	6	7	8	9	10	11
	14	15	16	17	18	19	20		12	13	14	15	16	17	18
	21	22	23	24	25	26	27		19	20	21	22	23	24	25
	28	29	30	31					26	27	28	29	30		
June					1	2	3	**Dec.**						1	2
	4	5	6	7	8	9	10		3	4	5	6	7	8	9
	11	12	13	14	15	16	17		10	11	12	13	14	15	16
	18	19	20	21	22	23	24		17	18	19	20	21	22	23
	25	26	27	28	29	30			24	25	26	27	28	29	30
									31						

1 The Road to the Somme

Almost a century has passed since the First World War ended but the influence and effects of that war can still be seen today, especially in the Middle East, but also in Europe where the Balkans, which provided the spark that ignited the conflict, was re-shaped and has since seen further violence leading to another re-shaping and the redrawing of lines on maps.

In spite of the importance of the war in shaping the modern world, its memory has been distorted greatly in the popular mind and, if questioned about its history, most people would be able to mention only one or two battles. Foremost would be those battles that raged along the river Somme in the *department* of the same name. For many, 'the Somme' represents only a single day of battle, 1 July 1916, but this is a flawed perception, since the campaign, to describe it more accurately, raged until 19 November, by which time more than a million combatants had been killed or wounded. So it is that, while the name stands out in popular memory, understanding of what happened along the Somme is variable, to say the least.

In fact, the 1916 Battle of the Somme was not the sole encounter along that river, although it was the largest. The first Battle of the Somme had been fought between French and German forces in September and October 1914. Thus the 1916 battle was the second along that line and was followed by two more battles in 1918, the first in March as part of the final German offensive and the second in August as part of the *Entente* offensive that ended the war. To confuse matters even more, the British post-war Battle Honours Nomenclature Committee defined the 1918 battles as the First and Second Battles of the Somme; those of 1916 were described as 'Somme 1916'.

To place the 1916 campaign in its proper historical perspective, and examine why it was fought, it is necessary to look at the course of the war from

August 1914 until early 1916 for therein lie the reasons why British soldiers found themselves involved in battle in Picardie along the Somme. By the time the first British troops landed in France on 7 August 1914, German armies had already reached Liège in Belgium and the Belgian army was under severe pressure in trying to stop the German advance.

With the advantage of having taken the initiative, and with weight of numbers on their side, the German armies seemed unstoppable. Both the French armies and the newly-arrived Expeditionary Force from the UK were forced to cede ground and it seemed as if the Germans would reach and capture Paris. However, both French and British fought desperately and, although German aircraft bombed Paris on 30 August, no German troops were to reach the City of Light. The Belgians managed to stop the German advance on Antwerp by opening dykes and, in the first Battle of the Marne, French and British troops counter-attacked the invaders. It was the Germans' turn to retreat and the Entente pursuit continued in the Battle of the Aisne which ended on 28 September.

In Belgium the Germans seized Ypres and struck against Antwerp, which fell on 9 October. The Battle of Flanders, which included the First Battle of Ypres, ensued. Paris was bombed again, heavily, while Ostend and Zeebrugge were evacuated by the Entente and the Germans quit Reims. As fighting continued, the British forces, now titled the British Expeditionary Force (BEF), redeployed from the Aisne front to Flanders. Fighting on the Ypres front continued until 17 November with heavy loss of life on both sides.

The end of the Battle of Ypres was also the end of the war of movement. Exhausted, both sides began digging entrenchments that were to reach from the Channel coast to the Swiss frontier. Initially intended to provide temporary protection for troops before the renewal of more mobile warfare, these became permanent as the months passed and it became clear that the war on the Western Front had reached a stalemate. On the Eastern Front Germany and her ally Austria-Hungary had failed to inflict serious defeat on Russia but, with a much less restricted front, the war had not bogged down. The Germans had gained a new ally in Turkey which declared war on Britain and France on 12 November. Four days later, Mehmet V, Caliph of Islam, *Amir al Mu'minin*, Sultan of the Ottoman Empire and Keeper of the Two Holy Mosques, declared this to be a 'Holy War', or *Jihad*.

On the Southern Front the Serbian armies, pushed back by the invaders, had inflicted defeat on the Austrians who, by the end of the year, were preparing for a second invasion of Serbia. At Grahovo, Montenegrin forces had also compelled Austrian troops to retreat while Albanians, at the behest of Austria-Hungary, attacked Montenegro but were rebuffed. Thus, as 1915 opened, there was deadlock on the Western Front and no indication of any conclusive action on the other fronts. Nor did the war at sea offer any prospect of success to Imperial Germany and her allies, although German submarines had taken a heavy toll of Royal Navy ships and sailors, but a German naval victory off Coronel in Chile in early November was avenged by the Royal Navy in the Battle of the Falklands some weeks later.

Stalemate on the Western Front continued throughout 1915. Both sides launched offensives to break the deadlock but neither could bring to bear the overwhelming firepower and weight of numbers necessary for a break-in to become a breakthrough. In that year also, Italy joined the Entente and the Southern Front had a new definition as Austrian forces faced Italian along their common border.

During 1915 there was a major effort away from the Western Front to break the stasis. This was the attack on Turkey through the Dardanelles Strait, a strategy that grew out of French and British conviction that Turkey was weak and would soon crumble. However, Turkey proved much tougher than expected and the Entente troops committed to a land campaign on the Gallipoli peninsula (intended to allow a naval force to pass through to seize Constantinople) were bogged down quickly. An effort to reinforce the Mediterranean Expeditionary Force (MEF) in August also ended in stalemate and by December Entente troops were being evacuated, a process completed by 9 January. Many of the veteran units of Gallipoli would be redeployed to the Western Front where they would fight in 1916, some of the Irish units seeing action at the Somme as we shall note. There never had been sufficient strength in the MEF to advance through the Gallipoli peninsula and reach Constantinople and certainly there was not the strategic wherewithal to take the city, even had it been reached. The campaign had been doomed before it even began.

One aim of the Gallipoli campaign had been to support Russia by knocking Turkey out of the war and opening a warm-water supply route to Russia.

At the political level an assumption that Germany's allies were propping up the German war effort had encouraged politicians in their decision to launch the flawed venture. Those politicians would continue to fail to recognise that Imperial Germany was propping up her allies and not *vice versa*; as a result there would be more sideshows.

The Entente commanders could not be accused of the same lack of vision as 1915 ended. On 6 December an inter-allied conference was convened at Chantilly. This was the second such 'summit' of commanders at Chantilly, the first having been held in July after Italy's entry into the war, and it was hosted and presided over by France's commander-in-chief (C-in-C), General Joseph Joffre, Chantilly being his headquarters. In attendance were senior officers from the UK, Russia, Italy and Serbia, who were presented with a proposal from the French for strategic inter-allied co-operation. The British representatives were led by Field Marshal Lord French, commander-in-chief of the BEF, and General Sir Archibald Murray, his chief of staff. (Murray had been commissioned in the 27th (Inniskilling) Regiment in 1879, while French, ennobled as Lord French of Ypres and of High Lake in the County of Roscommon, came of Irish stock and would be the last Lord Lieutenant of Ireland.)

Two days before the Chantilly Conference, Field Marshal Lord Kitchener, the British war minister, who had already ordered the abandonment of the Gallipoli campaign, had met French representatives, led by prime minister Aristide Briand, at Calais and persuaded them to abandon the campaign in Salonica, which was absorbing manpower and *matériel* to no strategic purpose – as with Gallipoli, the war was never going to be won in Salonica. The French agreed reluctantly. However, there was public outcry in France about the decision which Joffre used to persuade the British delegation at Chantilly to reverse the previous decision, for fear of destabilising Briand's government, and continue the Salonica campaign to ensure that Greece would not be overrun.

The Russian representative, General Yakov Zhilinski, was keen to promote greater strategic co-operation and advised the other Entente commanders that the Russian chief of staff, General Mikhail Alexeev, would be ready to take part in a combined Entente offensive in 1916. At this stage, Germany and her principal ally, Austria-Hungary, were fighting on three main fronts in Europe: on the Western Front, German forces faced French and British troops with the rump of the Belgian army still in the fray;

on the Eastern Front the foe was Russia and on the Southern Front Austro-Hungarian forces faced Italian armies in northern Italy while conflict still raged in the Balkans. Thus the Entente commanders developed the concept of co-ordinated offensives to bring to bear the maximum pressure possible on the Central Powers, making it difficult for them to switch formations from threat to threat on the different fronts. This plan was the genesis of the Somme campaign of 1916. It also contained an agreement that should any of the allies be threatened by enemy offensives, the others would react at once with diversionary operations. This may have presaged the concept of NATO but it also had the potential for an adverse effect on the grand plan: inevitably such diversionary operations could be initiated quickly by the premature launch of one of the planned offensives, thereby diluting the overall strategy. And so it was to be, with Germany taking the initiative in this respect early in 1916.

Second meeting of the Entente Council of War, March 1916. From left to right: General Castelnau of France, Sir Douglas Haig of the United Kingdom, General Wielemans of Belgium, General Zhilinski of Russia, General Joffre of France, General Porro of Italy and Colonel Pechiych of Serbia.
From *L'Illustration* 1916

Pictorial Press/Alamy

SOMME

21 FEBRUARY 1916
Germans launch attack on the French frontier town of Verdun with the intention of wearing down the French armies. This reduces the French commitment to the strategic offensive on the Western Front – British commitment is increased to compensate.

24 JUNE 1916
BATTLE OF THE SOMME begins with opening of a planned 5-day bombardment.

DECEMBER 1915	JANUARY 1916	FEBRUARY 1916	MARCH 1916	APRIL 1916	MAY 1916	JUNE 1916

6 – 8 DECEMBER 1915
CHANTILLY CONFERENCE
Entente commanders from France, the UK, Russia and Italy meet at General Joffre's headquarters at Chantilly to discuss a French proposal for co-ordinated offensives against the Central Powers in 1916. Field Marshal French represents Britain but, shortly afterwards, is succeeded by General Haig as Commander-in-Chief of the British Expeditionary Force.

MARCH 1916
Russia launches the Lake Naroch offensive to ease pressure on the French. The offensive fails with disastrous effects on Russian morale. Italy launches inconclusive offensive across the Isonzo river on the Southern Front.

4 JUNE 1916
Russia launches the Brusilov offensive on the Eastern Front – meets with considerable success. After a speedy breakthrough, during which Austria-Hungary's Archduke Josef Ferdinand narrowly escapes capture, Russians reach the Carpathian mountains. The offensive dies down in late September. Although it forces the Germans to call off the siege of Verdun and brings Romania into the war against the Central Powers it does not draw sufficient German forces from the Western Front to allow the Western Entente armies to achieve success on the Somme.

PHASE ONE

PHASE TWO

PHASE THREE

Battle of Flers-Courcelette
15 – 22 SEPTEMBER

Battle of Albert
1 – 13 JULY

Battle of Morval
25 - 28 SEPTEMBER

Battle of Bazentin Ridge
14 – 17 JULY

Battle of Thiepval Ridge
26 – 28 SEPTEMBER

JUNE 1916	JULY 1916	AUGUST 1916	SEPTEMBER 1916	OCTOBER 1916	NOVEMBER 1916

Battle of Fromelles
19 – 20 JULY

Battle of le Transloy
1 OCTOBER – 11 NOVEMBER

Battle of Delville Wood
14 JULY – 5 SEPTEMBER

Battle of the Ancre Heights
1 OCTOBER – 11 NOVEMBER

Battle of Pozières Ridge
23 JULY – 7 AUGUST

Battle of the Ancre
13 – 18 NOVEMBER

Battle of Guillemont
3 – 6 SEPTEMBER

28 JUNE 1916

Bad weather causes delay until 1 July. The infantry are to make their assault on 29 June but are delayed due to the weather: the bombardment continues.

Battle of Ginchy
9 SEPTEMBER

19 NOVEMBER 1916

General Haig closes down operations on the Somme.

General Sir Douglas Haig

General Sir Douglas Haig succeeded Field Marshal Sir John French as Commander-in-Chief of the BEF in December 1915, inheriting the British element of the Entente's planned summer offensive in 1916. He tried, but failed, to have the offensive delayed so that the BEF's infantry might benefit from more training, and to allow the artillery to increase the numbers of guns and its ammunition stocks.

Haig has been criticised for the high casualty levels in his campaigns with one American military history magazine calling him the 'worst general' of the war, while the soubriquet 'Butcher' has also been applied to him. Lloyd George, who became prime minister in 1916, was highly critical of him, yet never replaced him as C-in-C, although he denied Haig many reinforcements who could have helped stem the German spring offensive of 1918. There was no one who could take his place.

Among criticisms levelled at him, Haig has been accused of being unable to understand modern tactics and technology, as well as being class-bound and incompetent. The truth is that Haig encouraged innovation, his use of tanks at Flers-Courcelette being an example of this. He was an enthusiast for the tank, as he was for the use of aircraft, having shown a keen awareness of the potential of aircraft early in the war, meeting with Major Hugh Trenchard of the Royal Flying Corps to organise aerial photography of the German lines; Haig also saw the value of aircraft for directing artillery fire. Aware of the unpreparedness of many of his divisions in early 1916 and, realising that he had no option but to attack, he increased the level of training and planned the offensive so that the infantry could have the best possible support from the artillery, reinforcing divisional artillery strengths in some instances with French regiments on loan – 36th (Ulster) Division was one formation that included a French artillery regiment. The training prior to the Somme offensive also introduced new weapons, such as the Lewis gun, Stokes mortars and hand grenades (the last in place of the improvised bombs used earlier) with revised tactics to take advantage of these innovations.

In spite of Lloyd George's criticisms, including the comment that Haig was a soldier 'to the top of his polished boots', his soldiers admired and respected him, as is indicated in surviving contemporary diaries. The proof of his abilities lies in the BEF's providing the engine of the Entente advances from 8 August 1918 that led to the Germans seeking the armistice that began on 11 November. Professor Gary Sheffield describes this as the 'greatest military victory in British history' while the American General Pershing described Haig as 'the man who won the war'.

Haig died in 1928, having spent much energy in his final years looking after the welfare of his former soldiers, through the British Legion, the creation of the Haig Fund to provide financial aid for ex-servicemen, and Haig Homes, to provide housing for them. His state funeral in London (his body had lain in state in St Columba's Church, Pont Street, London) was attended by massive crowds, many of them ex-soldiers whom, *The Times* noted, had 'come to do honour to the chief who had sent thousands to the last sacrifice when duty called for it, but whom his war-worn soldiers loved as their truest advocate and friend'.

2 The Western Front 1916

The plan developed for the Western offensive in 1916 placed the main burden of operations on the French armies. Field Marshal Sir John French, who had represented the UK at Chantilly, was shortly afterwards relieved of his command and succeeded by General Sir Douglas Haig. Although the British involvement was to be as the junior partner, Haig was concerned greatly about both the timing and location of any offensive involving his armies. Well aware that the majority of his soldiers were now wartime volunteers, and not fully trained, he wanted more time to complete their training and he would also have preferred British operations to be on or near the Channel coast, ensuring that communications with Britain were protected. Haig also believed that the proposed timing of late June for the Franco-British offensive was too early for the inexperienced British forces. He would have preferred a date later in the summer but had to fall in line with the French plans. But those plans were going to be changed by force of circumstance four months before the planned offensive.

On 21 February 1916 the Germans launched a major attack on the French frontier aimed at Verdun-sur-Meuse, in Lorraine. General Erich von Falkenhayn, the German chief of staff, aimed to strike a major blow at the French to capture Verdun which formed a salient open to attack from three sides. The city's defences had been reduced since the outbreak of war, thus making it an easier target. However, French resolve, summed up in the cry *'ils ne passeront pas'* (they shall not pass), led to one of the most costly battles of the war.

Commanding French Second Army at Verdun was General Philippe Pétain, who, in the course of the battle, was promoted to command Army Group Centre, which included fifty-two divisions. Pétain chose not to keep his infantry divisions in the battle continuously, as did the Germans. Instead, he used a roulement deployment, rotating divisions on a fortnightly basis. He also maintained a supply route from Bar le Duc along which lorries towed artillery and carried ammunition, supplies and fresh troops to the besieged town. This route became known as *la Voie Sacrée*. Pétain's organisation, and his skilled use of artillery, played a major role in wearing down the German offensive which ground to a standstill in July, although fighting continued until December.

While Pétain had stopped the German onslaught he had also played into Falkenhayn's hands, since the latter's intention was to wear down the French armies. That had certainly been the case, but the Germans had also lost heavily. Such was the attrition on both sides at Verdun that the French had to reduce their involvement in the summer offensive, forcing the British to assume a greater proportion of front than intended originally. Falkenhayn had intended to split the Franco-British alliance in 1916 before the Entente could build up its *matériel* superiority to the point where it would be unbeatable, but had failed to do so and would be relieved from his post as a result.

The battle of attrition at Verdun forced Franco-British commanders to reduce their expectations for the planned offensive in late June. This was no longer to be a decisive battle but one intended to relieve pressure on Verdun, keep German divisions in France and help the Russians in the Brusilov offensive on the Eastern Front. Launched in early-June, the Brusilov offensive drew in German formations that had been due to transfer to the Western Front. Such were the casualties sustained at Verdun that the French contribution to the new offensive had to be reduced. The British Fourth Army, formed on 1 March 1916 under Lieutenant General Sir Henry Rawlinson, would take the main burden of the attack: twenty British and thirteen French divisions were to deploy along the front.

By now the other nations of the Entente had undertaken their offensives. Russia's Brusilov offensive has been mentioned, but Russian forces had also launched an offensive in March 1916 which had been a spectacular failure. Initiated, at Joffre's request, to help the French, the Lake Naroch offensive had cost many Russian lives and seriously damaged morale in the Tsar's armies. However, it was the Brusilov offensive, in modern Ukraine, that was Russia's contribution to the Entente's grand strategy – and the finest Russian feat of arms of the entire war. Opened on 4 June, not only did it contribute to breaking the German attack on Verdun but it continued throughout the summer, ending in September and bringing Romania into the war on the side of the Entente. However, as many as a million Russian casualties were suffered in probably the costliest offensive of the war; it was also one of the costliest in history. Added to earlier losses, this contributed to the eventual collapse of the Russian armies in 1917.

On the Southern Front Italy's contribution to the grand plan was an attack across the Isonzo river which began on 9 March and lasted until the 16th. This, the fifth offensive along this line, was launched as a distraction to shift the Central Powers' attention from the Eastern Front and from Verdun. The Italian commander, General Luigi Cadorna, had Second and Third Armies under his command, which included eight fresh divisions. He intended to take Gorizia and the Tolmin bridgehead, but bad weather brought the offensive to an end with the loss of about 4,000 lives on either side; some small actions, usually at sub-unit level, continued until the end of the month but there was no clear winner in this clash. In June an Austrian surprise attack was repelled and Italian armies counter-attacked with some success, once again fighting along the Isonzo.

Only the offensive on the Western Front remained. With a planned starting date of 29 June, the British-French offensive was intended to further wear down the German armies, forcing them to concede ground. Meanwhile, von Falkenhayn had appreciated that there would be a counter-offensive against his attack on Verdun, but still believed that the French would be ground down and that any British attack could be repelled easily, allowing German armies to deliver the final punch that would force the Entente to the negotiating table. What the Germans considered a great naval victory at Jutland (in reality, a strategic defeat for the German *Hochseeflotte*) boosted German morale, especially on the home front. Although, by June, the German High Command (*Oberste Heeresleitung* or *OHL*) were beginning to recognise that the French army had not been beaten at Verdun, they still considered that they would be incapable of any counter-offensive, leaving such action to their inexperienced British allies. Thus, it was felt, any Entente offensive could be beaten off with little difficulty.

3 The Build Up: Planning and Preparation

Considerable preparations were being undertaken by the BEF and the French armies. These included intensive training of the formations and units that would assault the enemy lines; sapping to enable the laying of mines under the German positions to support the assault; improvements in logistical provision; and the build-up of artillery and ammunition. Above all, it was essential to have the best possible information on the enemy's positions and the disposition of his troops while denying him similar intelligence on Entente formations.

The critical intelligence element of the preparation involved several aspects. Information from a network of agents behind enemy lines helped create a picture of troop movements and the dispositions of reserve formations. During June reports confirmed that the Russian offensive was drawing off German troops as troop trains steamed eastwards, reducing the reserves available to German commanders on the Western Front. At the end of the month the French *Deuxième Bureau* estimated German strength at 121 infantry divisions with nineteen reserve divisions. Of the latter, seven were behind the Somme front, five of them facing the British sector, while the others could be brought in from elsewhere on the front. In fact, there were only ten German reserve divisions, with six behind the Somme. Those German formations faced 157 Entente divisions, of which fifty-four were British and the remainder French.

While the French overestimated German reserve strength behind the Somme front, Haig's intelligence staff produced an underestimate, suggesting that there were only nine German reserve divisions in the west, three of them behind the Somme front. Moreover, the three divisions behind the Somme were assessed as being of inferior quality, a judgement that was to have unfortunate ramifications in the operational planning. As Haig assumed command of the BEF, the chief of intelligence,

Brigadier General George Macdonogh, was recalled to London to become Director of Military Intelligence (he had been head of the War Office's intelligence division until the outbreak of war). His successor in the BEF, Brigadier General John Charteris, who became known as Haig's 'evil counsellor', was not trained in military intelligence and was responsible for a number of over-optimistic intelligence assessments. However, Haig did not trust Macdonogh, who criticised some of Charteris's work (even calling him 'a dangerous fool'), but was later forced to replace Charteris. It seems that Haig's distrust of Macdonogh was based on the latter being a Catholic who had converted from Methodism (a Royal Engineer, Macdonogh had also been called to the Bar and was a skilled linguist, fluent in several languages).

Intelligence was also gathered by listening in to German telephone calls. To do this, listening posts were established but it was discovered that the Germans had a more effective telephone interception system, which alerted them to some of the plans for the assault and enabled them to prepare their response. Further information was gathered through the interrogation of prisoners and the British Army had created a new Intelligence Corps for that purpose in 1914. The interrogators, skilled linguists, questioned prisoners taken in trench raids and deserters to form a picture of German morale, unit strengths and activity. Similar practices were also in place in the French armies. Added to this information was that gained from ground-based observation posts, created by battalions and their commanding brigades and divisions. On the Somme front, for example, the foremost German defensive line was on the forward slope of the Thiepval ridge, allowing observers in the British line, across the valley of the Ancre river, to watch activity in the line and assess the strength of the defences.

Aerial observation played a critical role in building the overall intelligence picture since airborne observers could see behind the enemy's front line. Aircraft and balloons were used by both sides, the latter being especially vulnerable since they were tethered. (The German *Drachen* balloons were targeted by Entente airmen on 25 June so that they could not provide information to their artillery that would enable them to fire at the allied gun positions.) The slow observation aircraft were defended by 'scout', or fighter, machines as they flew over and behind the front. Aircraft enabled the Entente forces to look behind the German front lines while the forward German positions were often located on high ground, giving them clear observation of the Franco-British lines. In particular, the entire British front on the Somme was overlooked by German positions on the Thiepval spur, which enabled German artillery to target any section of the British line. However, the eyes in the air provided by the Royal Flying Corps (RFC) were performing the same task for the Entente with cameras producing images of the German artillery lines and rear areas. Such reconnaissance allowed Haig's staff to produce a good map of the German second defensive line and their gun positions. It also revealed that the third line was but a shallow trench for the most part. Aware of the ability of the Entente to observe from the air, the Germans took precautions to diminish the intelligence that could be gained by deploying fighter aircraft to seek out the slow observation planes while, on the ground, every effort was made to dig in and camouflage guns and other positions. Although wireless sets were fitted in some observation aircraft, these were fairly basic and capable only of transmitting; the ground stations that received the messages had to relay them to the artillery batteries by landline. However, by the end of the war the equipment and the system would have improved beyond recognition, allowing much faster communication between airborne observers and guns. Significantly, the Germans considered that British infantry successes on the Somme in 1916 'were due to the superior co-operation between guns and aircraft'.

The artillery was already a major factor in planning and its role would become even more effective as the war progressed, with the fire plan for each operation the most complex element of that operation. However, there were problems in early 1916, which were part of Haig's rationale in wanting the offensive delayed. These problems fell into two linked categories: the supply of weapons and ammunition, and the re-organisation and enlargement of the artillery arm. As a small professional army, the pre-war British Army had an artillery arm – the Royal Regiment of Artillery – that matched its size and thus the BEF could not bring to bear a weight of artillery comparable to those of their French allies and German foes, each of whom had large conscript armies.

When war broke out in 1914 the Royal Artillery was organised in three discrete elements: the Royal Horse Artillery (RHA), the elite of the Army, which was intended to deploy quickly and thus used 13-pounder light guns; the Royal Field Artillery (RFA), whose role was to support the army in the field; and the Royal Garrison Artillery (RGA), which manned fixed defences across the UK and the Empire. Since the field armies possessed

16

very little heavy artillery, units of the RGA deployed to the Western Front to man heavy guns and howitzers that were usually positioned some distance back from the lines.

The basic equipment of the RFA was the 18-pounder gun. Horse-drawn, it had a maximum range of just over 6,500 yards. These guns were deployed in six-gun batteries, which had been reduced to four-gun units by 1916 (they were later restored to their original strength), with three batteries forming an artillery brigade under command of a division. Re-organisation within artillery brigades meant that each included a 4.5-inch howitzer battery in place of one of the 18-pounder batteries; this weapon's maximum range was 7,300 yards and it fired a 35-pound shell. By June 1916 a typical infantry division deployed fifty-four 18-pounders and twelve 4.5-inch howitzers while each division had also lost an artillery brigade to allow 'Army Brigades' to be formed; these were available to army commanders to enable effective concentration whenever and wherever firepower was needed.

A 12-inch howitzer of the Royal Garrison Artillery ready for action during the opening phase, in the Battle of Albert. By 1 July 1916 the BEF had 11 of these howitzers, plus six of the heavier 15-inch weapons.

© Imperial War Museums (Q 1537)

A 4.5-inch howitzer in action during the early stages of the campaign.

RGA batteries were equipped with a range of weapons, including the heaviest gun used by the British forces, the 60-pounder, which could engage targets well behind the enemy lines. There were also two howitzers that fired heavier rounds than the 60-pounder: these were the 8-inch with a 200-pound round and the 9.2 with a 290-pound round; their ranges were over 10,000 yards, as was that of the 60-pounder, although the latter was modified to fire to over 12,000 yards and, later, 15,500. A modified naval 6-inch gun, firing a 100-pound shell, was also used by the RGA and had a slightly greater range than the heavier weapons. Together with 6-inch howitzers these weapons were held in corps-level artillery units of the RGA with a desired complement of twenty-four 60-pounders, sixty 6-inch howitzers and twenty-four 8- or 9.2-inch howitzers in a three-division corps; irrespective of corps size, only eight 6-inch guns were available. By the time of the Somme campaign some railway guns were available and some 12-inch and 15-inch howitzers.

However, the proportion of heavy weapons to light in the BEF in June 1916 was much less than was needed on a large battlefield. This was a major disadvantage, exacerbated by an overall shortage of guns and ammunition. Before the war all the Royal Artillery's ammunition for guns and howitzers was produced by the Royal Ordnance Factories (ROF), but the massive expansion to fight a large-scale war in Europe and elsewhere was something with which the ROF could not cope and, although production was increased,

8-inch howitzers
of 39 Siege Battery RGA
in action at Fricourt
during the battle.

quality suffered and the factories were stretched to breaking point. Most ammunition held by the Royal Artillery was shrapnel which was effective against troops in the open and in colonial warfare but could not inflict damage on dug-in positions. The British Army needed what the German army had in plenty – high explosive (HE) ammunition. In 1914 HE ammunition was produced only for howitzers and the explosive used, Lyddite, was not the most reliable, as well as being difficult to detonate. Not until Amatol, a mixture of TNT and ammonium nitrate, was a reliable explosive found and shells could be filled with HE.

This 12-inch railway gun was in action before and during the campaign. Its presence near the lines of 109 Brigade of the Ulster Division was noted by Jim Maultsaid of 14th Royal Irish Rifles since its use brought German retaliatory fire down on the division's positions.

The lack of HE shells was not the sole problem in what was dubbed the 'shell scandal'. The RFA went to war in 1914 with only shrapnel shells and a simple timed fuse. A new fuse was needed for HE rounds and so the No.100 Fuse was devised but this had a difficult gestation with a spate of rounds detonating prematurely in the barrels of weapons. At first this happened with the RFA's 4.5-inch howitzers and so many men lost their lives that 4.5 detachments were nicknamed 'suicide clubs'. The problem spread to 18-pounders and even to 9.2-inch howitzers, while mishandling of ammunition in dumps led to two major explosions that cost many lives. Of the rounds discharged it was believed that many never exploded, the effects of which on the opening of the Somme campaign we shall see.

In May 1915 David Lloyd George was appointed Minister of Munitions and his energetic and organised mind soon set to work to solve the problem. Private industry was brought into the ammunition production process and Lloyd George took over responsibility for designs and inventions from the Master General of the Ordnance in November. Although it would take time for all the problems to be resolved, the supply of weapons and ammunition began to improve. Even so, Field Marshal Haig wrote in his final *Despatch* of 21 March 1919 that 'It was not until mid-summer 1916 that the artillery situation became even approximately adequate to the conduct of major operations', going on to note that, throughout the Somme campaign, ammunition expenditure had to be carefully controlled. He commented that not until 1918 was the artillery free of 'any limiting consideration other than that of transport'.

When all the plans had been laid and the artillery had completed their bombardments, it would be up to the infantry to cross no man's land and seize ground from the enemy. The guns would still be available to support them, but the greatest burden would fall on the PBI, the poor bloody infantry. In what was a new form of warfare, pitting the industrial might of highly-developed nations against each other in massive armies, very careful thought had to be given to how the infantry could operate, and plans for the most effective use of infantry had to be formulated.

Contrary to popular belief, the opposing lines were not simple single linear trenches but were carefully-devised defensive positions designed to inflict the maximum hurt on any attacker. Since the Entente forces had

View from the old British trenches. Painted by Sir William Orpen in 1917, this is a view over landscape torn by battle. Patches of grass are growing out of the mud and an overgrown trench is in the foreground. The fields in the distance are shadowed by heavy clouds above. Orpen, born in County Dublin, was commissioned in the Army Service Corps and travelled to France in 1917 where he created a series of sketches and paintings, of which this is one. He was later knighted and became a member of the Royal Academy.

dug in at the end of an offensive there was a feeling in the British command that these positions were temporary, to be held only until the armies moved forward in the next advance. However, the Germans, having dug in at the end of a withdrawal, had expected further assault by the Entente and so had created more formidable defensive positions, made even stronger by the fact that their withdrawal had left them, in many areas, on ground overlooking their foes' positions. Although both British and French armies improved and strengthened their positions, so that they provided protection in depth, the Germans had gone further, digging deeper into the ground, creating elaborate systems reinforced with concrete and given overhead cover that was proof against a direct hit from a 60-pounder and could even stand up to a series of heavy strikes.

Barbed wire, patented in the United States shortly after the Civil War as a means of enclosing cattle, was laid in deep coiled belts, known as concertina wire, in front of the first line of trenches – the fire trenches – and was a major obstacle for attacking infantry. First used in the Spanish-American War and then in the Boer and Russo-Japanese wars, destroying barbed wire was a task given to the artillery, as we shall see, while infantry soldiers could use trench mortars, wire-cutters or Bangalore

Trenches

Trenches will be forever associated with the First World War since most of the war on the Western Front was fought between foes locked into extensive trench systems. Although beginning as one of movement, the war had stagnated into static fighting by October 1914 and remained as such until August 1918 when, once again, it became a war of movement.

Trenches were not new. They had been used in the Boer War, the Russo-Japanese War, the American Civil War and the Crimean War. Wellington's famous Lines of Torres Vedras, the shield for Lisbon in the Peninsular War, were trenches and fortresses built by his engineers. The pre-war *British Field Service Regulations and Infantry Training 1914* had included instructions on how to site and construct trenches.

At first trenches had a temporary appearance but gradually became more sophisticated with a permanent look, especially on the German side. Since the Germans were dug in on French or Belgian soil, the Entente armies had to take the offensive to remove them. This is one reason why German trenches on the Somme and elsewhere were so sophisticated, even including deep concrete dug-outs offering excellent protection from heavy artillery fire.

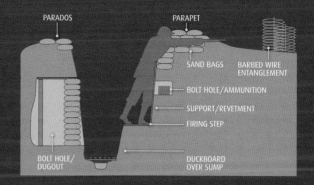

The chalky soil of the Somme required strong support, although it was well drained. Drainage was important as soldiers tried to keep their feet as dry as possible to avoid trench foot. Interestingly, the first unit to use duckboards in an effort to keep feet dry was the 1st Battalion of the Royal Irish Fusiliers. The sketches include a typical trench layout in 1916, showing how the defensive system was 'layered', and a cross section of a trench. There were variations in layout, depending on the ground (in the wet ground of Flanders 'trenches' were often built up rather than being sunk into the soil), but these are appropriate to the Somme.

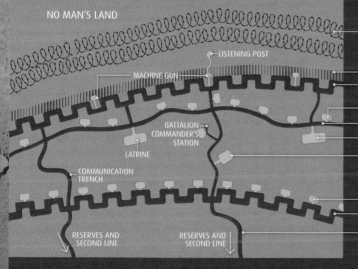

As the months passed the trenches became defensive systems. Rather than being single lines, they expanded into zones providing strength in depth. The first German defensive zone on the Somme included three discrete lines of trenches with two further defensive zones. Such defences made a breakthrough extremely difficult for any attacker.

A common image of the war is that infantry soldiers spent most of their time in trenches, 'up to [their] necks in muck and bullets', but nothing could be further from the truth. The typical tour of duty in the front-line trenches was four days, after which the defending units would move back; battalions could spend a month or more behind the front. There were occasions when circumstances demanded that a battalion spend longer in the front-line trenches but these were exceptions.

22

torpedoes. At first barbed wire had been laid in fence form but before long soldiers had developed concertina wire[1], a more effective obstacle that could be laid using steel pickets rather than wooden posts. Initially, wire obstacles were about ten yards deep but this soon increased threefold with its effectiveness increased by siting trip wires to set off flares or warning guns when disturbed. Simplest of all, tin cans, available in plenty, could be hung from trip wires to provide warning of the approach of an enemy under cover of night.

Bangalore Torpedo

The Bangalore torpedo was developed at Bangalore in India in 1912 by an officer of the Madras Sappers and Miners, Captain Robert Lyle McClintock, from Dunmore House, Carrigans, County Donegal. McClintock, a Boer War veteran, intended his invention to be used to explode booby traps and physical barriers left over from the Boer and Russo-Japanese wars.

The device, known popularly as the Bangalore torpedo, was adopted by the Army and used during the First World War to clear paths through barbed-wire obstacles. A simple piece of equipment, it consisted of a number of metal tubes, each about five feet (1.5m) long, screwed together like the rods of a chimney-sweep's brush. A torpedo could be fashioned to deal with various widths of belts of wire, with one or more tubes containing explosive charges.

To prevent snagging, a smooth nose cone was used. The torpedo could be pushed out from the protection of a trench, thus reducing the risk to the users.

During the Battle of Cambrai in 1917 Royal Engineers used Bangalore torpedoes to create a diversion to distract German attention from the location of the main attack. Other armies, including the US Army, adopted it and, although declared obsolete by the UK during the Second World War, it has continued in use ever since, although more modern developments are available. A modern Bangalore torpedo has been estimated to be effective for clearing a path through barbed wire or other obstacles, such as heavy undergrowth, up to 50 feet (15m) long and over three feet (1m) wide.

Robert Lyle McClintock retired from the Army as a colonel and died at Dunmore House, Carrigans, in 1943.

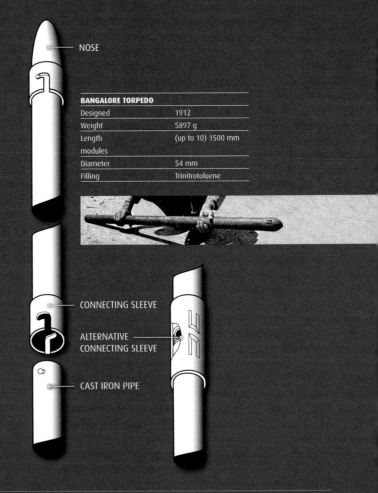

NOSE

BANGALORE TORPEDO	
Designed	1912
Weight	5897 g
Length modules	(up to 10) 1500 mm
Diameter	54 mm
Filling	Trinitrotoluene

CONNECTING SLEEVE

ALTERNATIVE CONNECTING SLEEVE

CAST IRON PIPE

---

[1] Now known as Dannert wire, after the German Horst Dannert who patented the concept in the 1930s.

Barbed-wire defences could be destroyed by artillery or mortar fire and
the infantry's Stokes 3-inch mortars, grouped in brigade mortar batteries,
were deployed with field artillery and mortars manned by the RFA, for
this task. Unfortunately, most of the rounds fired by the field guns were
shrapnel, which would not cut wire unless the round exploded in the
entanglements. The HE of the mortars was more effective and could cut
paths through the wire for the infantry. So too could the 75s of the
French artillery, some of which supported British formations, including
36th (Ulster) Division.

Following British and French offensives in 1915, and the German spring
offensive that became known as the Second Battle of Ypres, the immensity
of the task facing any attacker became ever clearer. At Neuve Chapelle
and Festubert in the spring, and Loos in the autumn, the British had
learned how important concentrated artillery fire was and the need to be
able to fight a battle in depth: in only a few minutes at Neuve Chapelle,
the British artillery had fired 15 per cent of all its ammunition stock in
France – and that was in the initial bombardment. Although British troops
had broken through the enemy line at Neuve Chapelle the Germans had
hastily organised reserves, and men from the broken line, to form a
second defensive line, which the attackers lacked the strength and artillery
firepower to crack. Likewise, at Vimy ridge the French found themselves
unable to break through while the British attacks at Aubers ridge and
Festubert were linked so closely with the French offensive at Vimy, the
second Battle of Artois, that they proved inflexible and failed, the former
proving the greatest setback to British arms thus far in the war. Loos
continued the pattern in September, and also led to French's replacement
as C-in-C of the BEF by Haig.

Critical lessons had been absorbed by both sides. British and French
commanders had found that it was possible to break in to the enemy's
lines, but that breaking through those lines and then breaking out onto
open ground was an altogether much more difficult proposition. For their
part the Germans, already aware of the importance of defence in depth,
had had this lesson emphasised. As a result, their positions along the
Somme which the British would have to assault on 1 July 1916 were much
stronger than those of 1915. Falkenhayn had initiated a construction
programme as far back as January 1915 and the Entente offensives of that
year had left no doubt about the necessity of the programme which was
in place by summer 1916. The earlier single barbed-wire belt, between five

24

This photograph of the entrance to a captured German dug-out at Montauban illustrates how well the Germans had prepared their positions. Dug-outs of such depth were immune to all but the heaviest artillery fire, and even then only a direct hit would have created major damage.

and ten yards wide, had been increased to two belts, each some thirty yards wide and about fifteen yards apart; each belt was also between three and five feet high. The first 'line' was no longer a single trench line but three distinct lines, between 150 and 200 yards apart: in the foremost trench were sentry troops, while the second (*Wohngraben*) line held the main body of the front-line garrison and the third was for local reserves. About 1,000 yards behind this first line of defence was the *Stützpunktlinie*, a series of strongpoints. From these lines, communication trenches led back to what had been the reserve line, but was now renamed the second line; this was built on the same principles as the first line and constructed and wired in the same fashion. The trench lines were traversed with sentry-posts in concrete recesses set into the parapet while the dug-outs had been deepened from the earlier six to nine feet to between twenty and thirty feet, with some as deep as forty; these dug-outs could hold up to twenty-five men and were set about twenty-five yards apart. To complicate matters further for an attacker, the second line was beyond the range of British and French field artillery, which meant that any attacking force would have to stop to allow the field guns to be brought forward to support an assault on that line. The third line was farther back, deeper in the defensive system, but, as aerial reconnaissance indicated, was far from complete. It will be noted that, although there were three defensive 'lines', there were many additional lines of trenches. Although it is claimed that the Ulster Division's leading troops reached the German fifth line on 1 July, the reality is that they were in the German *second* line. The confusion arises because the BEF command assigned the codes A, B, C and D lines to the four elements of the German first line.

Assaulting defensive positions held in such depth required a complex plan of attack involving artillery, engineers and infantry working in close co-operation, and drawing in other specialists to ensure logistic needs were met in the build-up and that the medical services were ready to deal with casualties. The deadlock on the Western Front equated to siege warfare in linear form and any attempt to break the stalemate required some aspects of that style of warfare. Engineers built light railways on which to carry supplies to the front; these could also be used to evacuate the wounded. Large stores, or dumps, of ammunition were brought forward for the field artillery and for the infantry's trench mortars. The engineers were also engaged below ground excavating tunnels leading towards the enemy lines. At the ends of these tunnels, mines were placed to be detonated as part of the assault plan, either to destroy specific

The Somme
1 July 1916

Foncquevillers

Ablainzevelle

Gommecourt

Bucquoy

Achiet le petit

Beugnâtre

Favreuil

Hébuterne

Puisieux

Biefvillers

Bapaume

Grévillers

Irles

Auchonvillers

Beaumont

Miraumont

Pys

Warlencourt

Ligny

Riencourt

RIVER ANCRE

Villers

Beaucourt

Grandcourt

Béaulencourt

le Sars

Hamel

Courcelette

Gueudecourt

Thiepval Wood

Thiepval

Mesnil

Martinpuich

Flers

Lesboeufs

Aveluy Wood

Pozières

High Wood

Morval

Authuille

Authuille Wood

Bazentin

Bouzincourt

Contalmaison

Bazentin le Petit Wood

Delville Wood

Ginchy

Aveluy

Bailiff Wood

Bazentin le Grand Wood

Longueval

Bouleaux Wood

RIVER ANCRE

la Boiselle

Mametz Wood

Guillemont

Leuze Wood

Combles

Shelter Wood

Caterpillar Wood

Montauban

Bernafay Wood

Trones Wood

Douage Wood

Becourt Wood

Fricourt

Albert

Mametz

Hardecourt

Maurepas

Carnoy

Maricourt

Curlu

Cléry

Suzanne

Bray

RIVER SOMME

SOMME CANAL

Legend
— German front line
— British front line
— Rivers/ponds
German ground
Marshes
Roads
Woods

0 1km 2km 3km 4km 5km

enemy strongpoints or to neutralise them by masking them with heaps of displaced soil and rubble. On the British front nineteen mines were laid; the scars on the landscape of one on the Hawthorn ridge, close to Beaumont Hamel, and two near la Boisselle may still be seen.

As all these preparations were being made, infantry units were training for their role. Even today the myth endures that, on 1 July 1916, British troops climbed out of their trenches and walked almost in parade-ground fashion across no man's land into the fire of German machine guns. Whilst III Corps' attack in the centre of the line used linear waves, most did not and there was a considerable degree of flexibility in Fourth Army's Tactical Notes with divisional commanders adapting their tactics to the ground over which their soldiers would have to fight and the objectives they sought. Perhaps the best example of this, as we shall see later, was Major General Nugent's plan for 36th (Ulster) Division's attack.

In the training of the infantry we see the rationale behind Haig's concern that the offensive was being mounted too early for the BEF. The army that had gone to war in 1914 had all but disappeared, with many of its soldiers killed or wounded while others had, perforce, been assigned to training the volunteers of the new armies being formed in answer to Kitchener's call for men. Conscription had been introduced in Great Britain in early 1916 but the first conscript soldiers had yet to arrive in France so that the early phases of the Somme campaign would be fought by volunteer soldiers. Many of the divisions that would fight on the Somme had little or no experience of combat, having arrived in late-1915 or early-1916. Among these were 16th (Irish) and 36th (Ulster) Divisions, which arrived before the end of the year; their soldiers therefore qualified for the 1914-1915 Star. Those who arrived in January 1916, such as 34th Division, raised in the north-east of England, and 35th Division, composed of men under the usual minimum height of 5 feet 3 inches, and therefore known as Bantams, did not qualify for the Star.

The infantry had to be trained for deep battle, with the attack force moving in waves, so that the first wave could break into and seize the first German position, with successive waves allowing the attack to move on against subsequent emplacements. To gain overall success, each unit had to be assigned a definite objective and had to know the enemy's dispositions in that area thoroughly. The French army had already developed such an attacking doctrine and knew that the maximum depth

Grenades

The earliest form of explosive grenade was used by Chinese armies of the Song dynasty between the tenth and thirteenth centuries AD, although incendiary grenades had been developed in the Byzantine Empire in the eighth century using *Greek fire*. However, the Chinese were the first to pack gunpowder into hollow metal or ceramic containers; they also developed the exploding artillery shell by filling hollowed cannon balls with gunpowder.

In Europe the grenade dates from the fifteenth century. The name appears to derive from the Spanish *granada* with *grenade* first coming into use in the British Isles in the wars following the deposing of King James II/VII. Although early weapons were not very effective, almost requiring a direct hit, they led to the introduction of grenadiers, or bombers, into infantry regiments and the creation of grenadier companies, distinguished by the wearing of a special cap resembling a bishop's mitre cap.

During the nineteenth century grenades re-appeared wherever trench warfare developed and there are accounts of improvised grenades being used by British soldiers in the Crimean War (1854–56). In the next decade the American Civil War (1861–65) saw a resurgence in their use with practical grenades developed by both armies.

The next conflict in which grenades were used was the Russo-Japanese War (1904–05) when the Russian defenders of Port Arthur improvised devices to use against the Japanese. This proved an embarrassment to the War Office which, in 1902, had decided that hand grenades had no place in modern warfare and declared them obsolete, a decision reversed less than two years later when the Board of Ordnance was ordered to develop a modern and practical hand grenade.

A number of grenades were devised but it was 1915 before British troops had an effective fragmentation bomb in the Mills grenade, which served the Army for many decades; its main design feature, a grooved surface similar to a chocolate bar, was thought to aid fragmentation but had no real effect, although it was retained in the design. The Mills grenade's seven-second delay fuse was well suited to trench warfare and it was the first modern fragmentation grenade.

The Mills bomb was adapted to be fired from a rifle: the previous Hales grenade had not been an effective or popular device. This gave the *bomber* a greater range while reducing his risk of being caught in the blast. In the early stages of the war, many soldiers improvised grenades from such items as jam-jars and pieces of metal and the introduction of the Mills grenade proved popular as well as allowing the re-introduction of the grenadier, or bomber, in the infantry section. Grenades were ideal in trench warfare.

Other nations also introduced hand grenades, the distinctive German stick grenade being one of the best known: the *Stielhandgranate* was also introduced in 1915, the stick allowing a longer range, up to 50 per cent, than arm power alone.

Some 75,000,000 grenades were manufactured in the UK during the war.

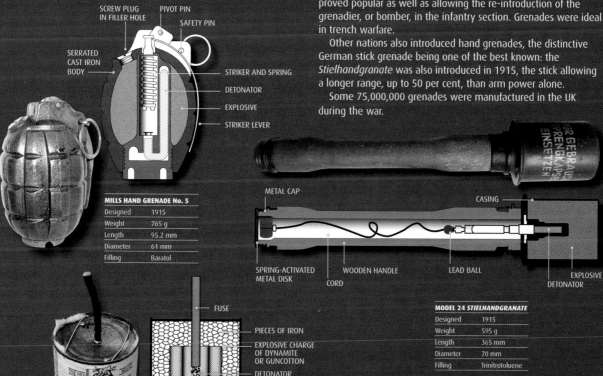

SCREW PLUG IN FILLER HOLE
PIVOT PIN
SAFETY PIN
SERRATED CAST IRON BODY
STRIKER AND SPRING
DETONATOR
EXPLOSIVE
STRIKER LEVER

MILLS HAND GRENADE No. 5	
Designed	1915
Weight	765 g
Length	95.2 mm
Diameter	61 mm
Filling	Baratol

FUSE
PIECES OF IRON
EXPLOSIVE CHARGE OF DYNAMITE OR GUNCOTTON
DETONATOR
JAM TIN BODY

METAL CAP
CASING
SPRING-ACTIVATED METAL DISK
WOODEN HANDLE
CORD
LEAD BALL
EXPLOSIVE DETONATOR

FÜR GEBRAUCH SPRENGKAPSEL EINSETZEN

MODEL 24 *STIELHANDGRANATE*	
Designed	1915
Weight	595 g
Length	365 mm
Diameter	70 mm
Filling	Trinitrotoluene

to which the infantry could penetrate was determined by the artillery's maximum range. French experience and this new doctrine were shared with their British allies; Rawlinson had sent staff officers to study French practice with infantrymen becoming specialists in one of the various elements of trench warfare, be that the rifleman with his rifle and bayonet, the bomber with his hand grenades, the rifle-bomber with a grenade-launching cup fitted to his rifle, or the light machine gunner. Fire-and-movement tactics, as practised by the pre-war Regular Army, were emphasised so that the battlefield might become more fluid with companies of infantry operating in smaller groups, each offering the other support. Such tactics were known to Fourth Army and were being practised: bombers and men equipped with rifle grenades, as well as light machine gun (LMG) teams and trench mortarmen were to take their place in the assaulting forces of Fourth Army. The LMG issued to British troops was the Lewis gun, which at 28lbs (12.7kg), was about half the weight of the Vickers and could be carried into action by infantry. Its availability played an important part in the changes being made in infantry tactics. With the advent of the Lewis, the Vickers guns, which had been brigaded in 1915, were taken over by the new Machine Gun Corps.

Another innovation in 1915 was the mortar. More accurately, it might be said that the mortar, around for centuries, was reintroduced as it had fallen out of favour during the nineteenth century (some elderly mortars were brought back into service when the utility of the weapon in trench warfare was realised). There were three categories of mortar: heavy, medium and light. The first two were operated by the Royal Artillery, but the light mortar was given to the infantry with each brigade having a battery of eight Stokes 3-inch weapons; the personnel were seconded from their own battalions. While effective, especially for cutting wire, the trench mortars were rarely favourites with the infantry since their use almost always meant counter-fire from their German equivalents, the *Minenwerfer*, or mine launcher.

It takes time to train soldiers in new tactics and every effort was made to conduct such training with battalions familiarising themselves with their objectives for Z Day on training areas that had been built to resemble as far as possible those they were to attack. However, Haig's concern about his inexperienced divisions and the need for more training time should be borne in mind: there was not enough time to train all the units of

Stokes Mortar

Mortars were first used by the Turks in 1451, during the siege of Constantinople when Mohamed II designed a 'new description of gun' that could destroy a ship by firing its shot to a great height so 'that in falling it might strike the vessel in the middle and sink her'. The word *mortar* is derived from a German word meaning *sea monster*.

Since the principle of the high trajectory shot was suited to siege warfare, mortars were adopted by armies across Europe. Usually fired from a *bed*, a basic wooden platform, the mortar was a short-barrelled weapon with little adjustment for elevation, range being controlled by adjusting the amount of powder in the charge.

The mortar fell out of favour after the Napoleonic wars but its utility was recognised as deadlock embraced the war on the Western Front with opposing armies facing each other from trenches across a narrow no man's land. Having learned lessons from the Russo-Japanese War the German army realised that a modern mortar was essential in any form of siege and the *Minenwerfer*, or mine launcher, was born.

On the British and French side, some very old mortars were removed from storage for use on the front. Meanwhile engineers in the UK set about developing new variants of the old weapon to give the Army a British answer to the *Minenwerfer*. Among designs submitted was one from Wilfred Stokes of the Ministry of Munitions' Inventions Branch for a simple mortar of 3-inch calibre (in fact, it was 3.2-inches or 81mm) with a smoothbore tube, or barrel, fitted to a base plate to absorb recoil and with a bipod mount. Initially Stokes' design was rejected since it did not fire existing British mortar ammunition but Lieutenant Colonel Matheson of the Trench Warfare Supply Department was impressed sufficiently to persuade the Minister of Munitions, Lloyd George, to approve the weapon for manufacture.

Once accepted for service, Stokes mortars were issued to infantry units and brigaded as trench mortar batteries (TMBs). By the opening of the Somme offensive the Stokes mortar was available in sufficient numbers to be a significant and effective weapon; its HE rounds cut wire better than the shrapnel of the field guns. A typical TMB had eight mortars, each manned by a two-man team, one to sight the weapon, the second to handle the ammunition. Rounds were dropped down the barrel where a primer on the base of the round would strike a firing pin to discharge it. Maximum range was about 800 yards (731m) with range adjusted by the number one mortarman changing the elevation (which varied between 45 and 75 degrees) or by using rounds with additional propellant rings.

A well-drilled mortar team could have a dozen rounds in the air at one time. So effective was the Stokes mortar that it remained in service until early in the Second World War. By November 1918 over 1,600 were being used by British and Commonwealth forces on the Western Front.

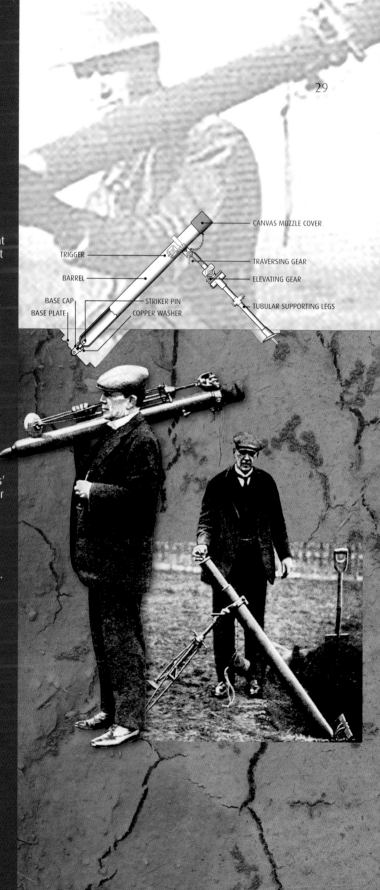

CANVAS MUZZLE COVER

TRIGGER

TRAVERSING GEAR

BARREL

ELEVATING GEAR

BASE CAP

STRIKER PIN

BASE PLATE

COPPER WASHER

TUBULAR SUPPORTING LEGS

Fourth Army to the levels necessary. The situation was exacerbated by the problems of the artillery. Those problems were not all obvious in the preparation period when it was not appreciated that as many as one shell in three was a dud, although there was a realisation that some shells were exploding prematurely, often with disastrous results.

The artillery fireplan was complex since it involved two major elements and a range of weaponry. Many problems faced the gunners but, on 5 June, the Major General Royal Artillery (MGRA) 'produced the first ever Army Artillery Operation Order. … and it was a masterpiece'. While the MGRA wanted to ensure that each corps' plan followed the same lines, tasks were defined, but not targets, and a six-day bombardment was ordered with co-ordinated pauses for aerial photography. Those weapons assigned to counter-battery tasks, i.e. neutralising the enemy artillery, had their tasks laid down. Deception plans were also co-ordinated but the allocation of guns to tasks, 'the tasks themselves, fireplans, observation and deployment were, quite rightly', left to corps artillery commanders. 'Massive stocks of ammunition' were built up, with seven trains a day bringing it forward, so that each 18-pounder had over 1,600 rounds available, each 6-inch howitzer had over 1,000 and each 8-inch howitzer had almost 600. Water and rations for six days were provided for each man and horse while 50,000 miles of telephone cable were laid, including 7,000 miles buried 6-feet underground to protect against German 5.9-inch shells. Aircraft were assigned to support the artillery, with four squadrons and a kite balloon squadron allocated to Fourth Army. Gridded maps, not available at the start of the war, were produced, marked in letter-coded squares, to assist aerial co-operation with the guns. Since the RFC controlled the skies, no German aircraft crossed over into British airspace during the preparatory period, 'perhaps the first really effective use of airpower in the land battle'.

> The tactics to be used were much discussed. The plan was that the Gunners should put down a massive barrage lifting forward at fixed times, with the assaulting infantry creeping forward as close behind it as they could get, at most one hundred yards, some said forty! The infantry were to move forward in waves. The first wave was not to mop up but to carry on to its objective, taking both its time and direction from the artillery. The fire was controlled by forward observers moving with the leading waves, reeling out cable as they went. Second waves were to mop up and secure objectives. These tactics were laid down by the general staff in a directive dated 16 May 1916, in which no mention was made of other tasks for the artillery; a second directive covered this …

Much thought was being given to the use of artillery which was to continue throughout the war, and the BEF's artillery would be a major factor in final victory. The French artillery of 1916 was even more sophisticated with a fireplan for Z Day that would hammer at the Germans' first position, allow the guns to register on the second position and support the infantry with a creeping bombardment regulated with precision. Impressive as the British artillery preparation was, it took second place to that of the French.

The French artillery enjoyed other advantages over their British counterparts. They could achieve a heavier concentration of fire, had a greater proportion of heavy weapons and did not have the problem of a high percentage of defective shells. In addition, the French made more effective use of their trench mortars, forming these into grand batteries to destroy enemy positions in the first line. On the French sector of the front the German positions were much closer – and therefore easier to observe – and were not held in the same strength as those facing the British, thus giving Sixth French Army another distinct advantage in the coming assault.

Infantry Battalion 1916

The infantry battalion is the standard building block of higher formations, such as brigades, divisions, corps and armies. In 1916 a British battalion numbered 1,007 men on paper but was often below that strength, usually due to casualties, illness, leave and training courses. In action the battalion would deploy about 800 men in four companies; each company included four platoons and each platoon four sections.

At battalion headquarters there were about 128 men, of whom 55 were the 'fighting portion' and 73 the 'administrative portion'. The former included the commanding officer (CO), second-in-command (2i/c), adjutant, the battalion Lewis-gun, signals and bombing officers, the regimental sergeant major (RSM), an orderly room clerk, two gas orderlies, 13 signallers, four stretcher-bearers, nine runners, 11 pioneers, two cooks and six batmen, or officers' servants. In the administrative portion were the assistant adjutant, quartermaster and transport officer, a quartermaster sergeant, two quartermaster storemen, a company quartermaster sergeant, seven storemen, 45 transport and grooms, three shoemakers, three tailors, two butchers, a postman, two cooks and three batmen.

In addition there were a medical officer (MO), chaplain and armourer, all 'attached' from their own corps. Every battalion had an Intelligence Officer, who was usually also in charge of snipers and scouts. A CO could add to the numbers in his HQ at his discretion to include additional stretcher-bearers, scouts or runners to the fighting portion and as many as 10 to the administrative portion.

Companies were commanded by captains, although this would change to majors, and a company HQ would include the commander, his second-in-command, a captain or lieutenant, a company sergeant major (CSM), a company quartermaster sergeant, four signallers, four runners (two of whom would also be batmen) and a cook. At a platoon HQ were the commander, a lieutenant, a sergeant, a signaller, a batman and a runner. Each platoon included four sections: two were rifle sections, one was a Lewis-gun section and the fourth a bomber section. Irrespective of role, a section was commanded by an NCO with nine soldiers. Other than the number one on the Lewis gun, every member of a section carried a rifle and bayonet; some men of the rifle sections were equipped with rifle grenade launchers.

BATTALION

IN ACTION

COMPANY ×4

= **PLATOON** ×16

= **SECTION** ×64

800

AT HEADQUARTERS

FIGHTING =55

ADMINISTRATION =73

ATTACHED =79

128

OTHER ROLES

79

TOTAL

1007

MAJOR
SECOND IN COMMAND
AND (LATER)
COMPANY
COMMANDER

SERGEANT
COMMANDED
SECTION

LIEUTENANT COLONEL
COMMANDED
BATTALION

LIEUTENANT
COMMANDED
PLATOON

CAPTAIN
COMMANDED
COMPANY

4 The Battle Opens: The Infantry's First Day

In February 1916 Foch and Haig had agreed that the initial infantry assault in the Somme offensive would be made on 1 July. This date, or Z Day, was later changed to 29 June, but the weather, in the form of heavy rain, intervened to force a delay until the original planned Z Day. As the training and preparation came to an end, formations and units moved to their assigned positions in readiness for the 'big push', as it had come to be known to British troops. Although the Germans expected a major Entente operation they had no idea of when it would begin, nor where the main thrust of the assault might occur. Since the RFC and the French Air Service denied them aerial surveillance over the front, German observers were limited to what they could see from ground observation and from tethered balloons – and, as noted already, Entente aircraft shot down those balloons on 25 June, using phosphorus bombs and, for the first time, le Prieur incendiary rockets. (Two days earlier, several British balloons had been struck and destroyed by lightning; the crew of another had a frightening experience when their balloon was torn from its winch and soared thousands of feet in a snow and electrical storm before, remarkably, one crewman managed to retrieve the situation.)

On 24 June the heavy guns began their work of knocking out the German batteries, a task in which they achieved considerable success: on the 26th nineteen enemy batteries were silenced, followed next day by another thirteen being hit, with many of them silenced, in spite of poor weather. Aerial observation on the 28th allowed thirty-two batteries to be engaged, even though many had been moved. Batteries north of Mametz and Montauban were all but annihilated, together with most of their ammunition, and German records noted that their 12th and 28th Divisions' artillery was wiped out by the 'devastating British artillery'. However, this success was not uniform across the front and there were

34

sectors where the German artillery survived in sufficient strength to rain devastating fire down on the attacking infantry.

On 27 June Major General Oliver Nugent, GOC of 36th (Ulster) Division, issued a Special Order of the Day to his soldiers. When he wrote that order he still expected the infantry attack to go in on the 29th although, also on the 27th, he wrote to his son, St George Nugent, that:

> I have a crow's nest sixty odd feet up in a tree from which I can see the German lines well back behind their front line and it is there I shall be sitting one day very soon, [author's italics] I expect, watching through my glasses the Ulster Division in advance to the assault.

The Ulster Division was to play a major part on 1 July but its infantry battalions were not the only Irish units involved. On the right flank of Nugent's men in X Corps were 2nd Royal Inniskilling Fusiliers in 96 Brigade of 32nd Division; 1st Inniskillings were in 29th Division of VIII Corps, on their left flank, serving in 87 Brigade with 1st Royal Dublin Fusiliers in 86 Brigade of the same division, while 1st Princess Victoria's (Royal Irish Fusiliers) and 2nd Royal Dublin Fusiliers formed half of 10 Brigade in 4th Division. Elsewhere, 2nd Royal Irish Regiment served in 22 Brigade of 7th Division in XV Corps and 1st Royal Irish Rifles in 25 Brigade of 8th Division in III Corps. A brigade of Tyneside Irish (103 Brigade, four battalions of Northumberland Fusiliers) formed part of 34th Division. In all, twenty Irish battalions, plus those Tyneside Irish, were to be committed to battle on 1 July; of the battalions of Irish Line Infantry, no fewer than seventeen were from the three Ulster regiments. Both 1st and 2nd North Irish Horse, in VII and X Corps respectively, were also assigned roles on Z Day, the former in VII Corps' diversionary attack at Gommecourt, but only to man a prisoner-of-war camp at Pas, the latter on various divisional tasks, such as escorting prisoners, manning control points and bringing forward bombs for the infantry's Stokes mortars.

The weeks before Z Day were busy for everyone but preparations were not helped by adverse weather: a cloudburst on 12 June made cross-country tracks impassable for infantry, impeded movement of ammunition to the new gun positions and made life unpleasant for men who had little shelter from the rain and spent several days in wet clothing. Late in the preparatory phase a French field artillery regiment was assigned to 36th (Ulster) Division to assist the divisional artillery and 11th Inniskillings

Major General Sir Oliver Nugent

Royal Irish Fusiliers Museum, Armagh

Major General Sir Oliver Nugent, the son of Major General St George Nugent and Emily, daughter of the Right Honourable Edward Litton, a senior judge and MP for Coleraine, was educated at Harrow and commissioned in the Royal Munster Fusiliers from the Royal Military College, Sandhurst, but transferred to the King's Royal Rifle Corps (KRRC) not long afterwards.

With the KRRC Nugent served in three expeditions on India's frontiers, the Hazara, Miranzai and Chitral campaigns. Mentioned in Despatches (MiD) for the Miranzai expedition, he received a further MiD for Chitral as well as being awarded the Distinguished Service Order (DSO), second only to the Victoria Cross as a gallantry award for a junior officer.

Nugent was promoted to major and served in South Africa in the Second Boer War where he was captured in the battle for Talana Hill. In August 1914 he was serving in Britain before, in 1915, being appointed to command 41 Brigade of 14th (Light) Division on the Western Front. In September he was appointed GOC of 36th (Ulster) Division and was promoted to major general on 1 January 1916.

Major General Nugent remained as GOC of the Ulster Division until 1918. It was he who decided that his leading soldiers would leave their assembly trenches before Zero Hour on 1 July to re-form along the sunken road, using that feature as their start line. As a result the first wave of the Ulster Division was able to overrun the German A Line and fight through to the Schwaben Redoubt. However, the Ulsters' advance had created a salient allowing them to be attacked on three sides and, with 108 Brigade's advance on the divisional left flank and 32nd Division's on the right being brought to a bloody halt by the German defence, there was no option but to withdraw.

This tablet was erected in Mountnugent Church, County Cavan, by General Nugent's fellow officers following his death in May 1926.

THIS TABLET IS ERECTED BY HIS BROTHER OFFICERS IN LOVING MEMORY OF
MAJOR-GENERAL
SIR OLIVER S.W. NUGENT, K.C.B. D.S.O.
WHO COMMANDED
THE 36TH (ULSTER) DIVISION 1915-1918
CALLED TO THE HIGHER SERVICE 31ST MAY 1926.
"AND GOD GAVE (HIM) WISDOM AND UNDERSTANDING AND LARGENESS OF HEART."
1 KINGS : 4 : 29.

Photo: Courtesy Major Richard Kilroy

were detailed to help them build shelters and dig gunpits 'with little enough time to do it'. This task was performed with zeal and:

> It seemed that they worked the harder because their work was for strangers, who would be left half-protected if they failed them. There was a fine flavour of international courtesy in the manner of their toil, for they gave of their freewill energy that not the most skilful of taskmasters could have wrung from them. General Nugent sent to Colonel Brush, then in command of the Battalion, a letter of warm congratulation upon their efforts.

The story of 36th Division on 1 July is well known, but the experiences of Irish units in other formations have been all but forgotten. Although five battalions of Royal Inniskilling Fusiliers, the Skins, fought on that day, the two regular battalions' stories are obscured by those of the three Inniskilling battalions in 109 Brigade of the Ulster Division. A similar fate has befallen 1st Royal Irish Rifles and 1st Royal Irish Fusiliers. Yet these battalions suffered heavily, as did the other Irish battalions in the actions of 1 July and subsequently.

The objective of the Ulster Division on that July morning was to capture the section of German front line between Thiepval village and the Ancre river, with six battalions, while a further two battalions across the Ancre were to seize enemy positions in ground on the fringe of the river valley. While the main attack was directed towards the Schwaben Redoubt (*Schwaben Fest*), one of the largest fortifications on the German front, the attack on the other bank of the Ancre was essential to protect the flank of the main effort. Two brigades were deployed along a frontage of 2,800 yards, 109 Brigade on the right and 108 on the left, the latter being 'split' by the river and its marshy valley. Nugent's third brigade, 107, was to follow behind 109, pass through the Schwaben Redoubt and press on to the German second line.

Nugent had decided that the divisional attack would not be launched from the assembly trenches but from a position partway between the lines. 'The sun came up in a clear blue sky; the artillery thumped away with unabated fury; trench mortars joined in; and it was Zero Hour.' Before Zero Hour, however, the leading companies moved into no man's land and lay down to await the lifting of the artillery bombardment. They had the advantage of being able to use a sunken road as cover. However, the move forward into the sunken road had another practical purpose. On this sector

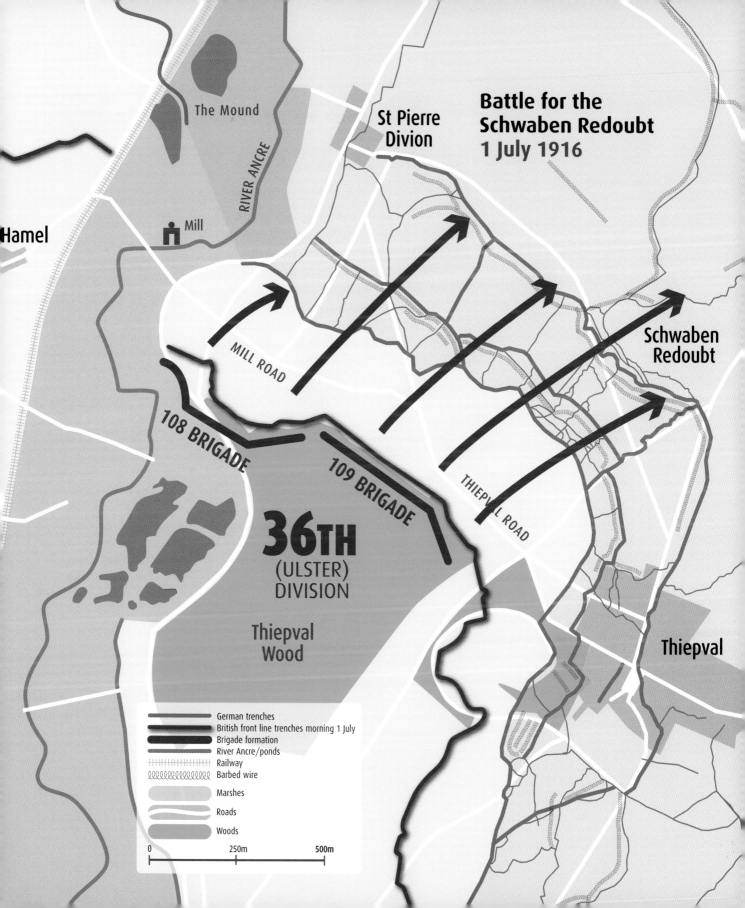

The Mound

St Pierre
Divion

**Battle for the
Schwaben Redoubt
1 July 1916**

RIVER ANCRE

Mill

Hamel

MILL ROAD

Schwaben
Redoubt

108 BRIGADE

109 BRIGADE

THIEPVAL ROAD

**36TH
(ULSTER)
DIVISION**

Thiepval
Wood

Thiepval

German trenches
British front line trenches morning 1 July
Brigade formation
River Ancre/ponds
Railway
Barbed wire
Marshes
Roads
Woods

0   250m   500m

of the front the opposing front lines were not parallel but diverged and so the attacking troops needed to re-form so that they were directed on the correct part of the German line. Since the sunken road was parallel to the German first line it also served the purpose of ensuring that the attackers were aligned correctly.

At Zero Hour two companies of each lead battalion, 9th (Tyrone) and 10th (Derry) Inniskillings, rose to their feet and made for the enemy front line. Thanks to the French 75s and the trench mortars, the wire had been cut effectively – not something that happened everywhere – and the Germans needed time to ascend from their deep dug-outs. Thus the foremost positions were overrun quickly after a brief but sharp encounter. The Derrys' commanding officer, Major Frank Macrory,[2] wrote of:

> The spectacle of these lines of men moving forward with rifles sloped and the morning sun glistening on their fixed bayonets, keeping their alignment and distance as well as if on ceremonial parade. ... this spectacle was not only impressive, it was extraordinary. Hardly a man was seen to fall at this stage of the advance.

Although there were few casualties at this stage, some were killed or wounded as they advanced. Those who followed up suffered more losses, either from the machine guns of Thiepval or the enemy artillery. Private Leslie Bell was in the second element of the Derrys, C and D Companies, to cross no man's land. Originally an under-age volunteer, his role was to carry a canvas bucket full of grenades for Private Duncan Jordan, a bomber. However, his platoon was no more than thirty yards into no man's land when a large shell burst above them, killing or wounding most of them. Bell was injured badly in the legs and lay for several hours before being rescued.

With a significant section of German line taken, it was time to send forward the next battalions, 11th (Donegal & Fermanagh) Inniskillings and 14th (YCV) Rifles, to consolidate the positions that had been seized. They also had to face the horrendous hail of machine-gun and artillery fire that swept no man's land.

Before these men had crossed no man's land a soldier of 36th (Ulster) Division had earned the formation's first Victoria Cross. The first of four

---

[2] Lieutenant Colonel Ross Smyth, the commanding officer, had recently been invalided home with a broken leg and was not to rejoin the battalion. He died close to his home when his trap overturned and he was thrown to the ground.

to be earned that day and the next, it was awarded posthumously to Lurgan man Private William 'Billy' McFadzean. Earlier that morning, in the assembly trench known as Elgin Avenue, in Bois d'Aveluy, soldiers of 14th Rifles were busy with their final preparations. As McFadzean, a 'bomber', opened a box of grenades, or bombs, it slipped from the ledge in the trench. Two bombs fell and their safety pins came loose. Knowing what would happen in such a confined space, McFadzean threw himself on the devices which exploded almost immediately, killing him. However, his swift reaction meant that only one other man was injured.

This photograph shows infantry crossing a trench. It was probably taken during training or staged for release to the press at home.

NAM. 1995-03-90-6
Courtesy of the Council
National Army Museum
London.

While General Haig could note in his diary that reports up to 8.00am were 'most satisfactory', and that British 'troops had everywhere crossed the enemy's front trenches', progress was soon to stall. The effects of enemy fire on units of 32nd Division, on the Ulster Division's right flank, had a catastrophic result for Nugent's men. Thirty-second Division, which included 2nd Inniskillings, had seen its attack falter almost as it had started with German machine guns in the ruined Thiepval village and the château on the Thiepval Spur taking their toll of the advancing infantry. Commanding officers of the attacking battalions withheld their last companies as they believed the attack had failed. With 32nd Division stopped the German machine gunners were able to switch their attention to the men of the Ulster Division, pouring fire into their right flank as they attempted to cross the old no man's land in front of Thiepval Wood. Added to that scourge was the tenacity of the Germans in the Schwaben Redoubt. Unlike their fellows in the first line, they had had ample warning of the attack and fought hard. One survivor of the Derrys recalled that the redoubt was bristling with machine guns and barbed-wire entanglements which caused major problems and led to many casualties. The attackers quickly found themselves being fired at from the front, both flanks and the rear, as many dug-outs had not been cleared in the speedy advance. Although British doctrine called for 'moppers up' to be deployed, such men were not trained to the same level as their French counterparts.

Thus 107 Brigade, with its three battalions of Royal Irish Rifles (the fourth was detached to 108 Brigade) not only had to move up through machine-gun fire from the Thiepval Spur and German artillery fire, but also had to join in the fight for the Schwaben Redoubt instead of passing through for the German second line. The Rifles did not use the sunken road to adjust their alignment, due to the machine-gun and artillery fire, and so their entry into the enemy line was not as planned. Some of the confusion and mixing of battalions during the battle for the Schwaben Redoubt can be attributed to this.

Many of 107 Brigade fell as the advance continued and one company commander, Major George Gaffikin, of 9th Royal Irish Rifles, rallied his soldiers, some of whom were hesitating, by waving either a piece of orange cloth or an orange handkerchief. In his book *The First Day on the Somme*, Martin Middlebrook claims that Gaffikin wore an Orange sash which he took off and waved, but this is mythology. Gaffikin's commanding officer, Percy Crozier, noted that it was a handkerchief. Gaffikin, from Ardglass, commanding B Company, was among the dead that day.

As 107 and 109 Brigades became more deeply embroiled in the battle for the Schwaben Redoubt, 108 Brigade's soldiers on the left flank were enduring their own horrific battle. The brigade's task was 'to clear the A and B lines within the [right centre] section, and advance to the C line, halting and consolidating on the salient C9, C10, C11, the north-east corner of the Schwaben Redoubt'. Three battalions of Irish Rifles were deployed on this task with the 11th on the right, 13th on the left and 15th, from 107 Brigade, in support. North of the Ancre the other two battalions of the brigade, 9th Royal Irish Fusiliers on the right and 12th Rifles on the left, were to attack the German salient to the left of the brigade objective, clear the trenches from there to the railway, establish strongpoints at B26,

The Bullet In The Bible

Private William Cordner of 9th Royal Irish Fusiliers was one of 600 men of his battalion who went into action on 1 July. A member of B Company, he was in the first wave of the attack on Beaucourt Station. (The start line for their attack is now Ancre Cemetery.) As they advanced, William's friends were cut down by machine-gun and shell fire, and he was knocked to the ground by a hard blow to his chest.

Although he picked himself up and moved forwards again, Private Cordner was knocked out by another explosion. Recovering consciousness in the dressing station that evening, he found that he had received a serious wound to his left arm. A devout Christian, he reached into his left breast pocket where he had a copy of *Daily Light*, a *New Testament* presented to him by his brother when he joined up in September 1914, aged 25, in Lurgan. Intending to read a piece of scripture, William discovered that his *Daily Light* contained a German bullet. The blow that had knocked him down had been the bullet hitting his chest. Its energy was absorbed by the little book. Without doubt its presence in his breast pocket had saved his life.

William Cordner was eventually discharged from the Army on medical grounds. Already married when war broke out, he had five children, three sons and two daughters. In civilian life he worked as a gardener, and as a school crossing patrol later in life. He rarely talked about his wartime experiences but the story of the 'Bullet in the Bible' was well known in Lurgan between the wars.

In 2006 William's *Daily Light* returned to the Somme. Colonel Hubert McAllister, the husband of one of his granddaughters, was Deputy Commander of 107 (Ulster) Brigade and carried the little book in the breast pocket of his uniform tunic.

The *Daily Light* carried by 14069 Private William Cordner, Royal Irish Fusiliers, in the breast pocket of his tunic on 1 July 1916 and the German bullet that lodged in it. The impact of the bullet knocked Private Cordner to the ground. Subsequently knocked unconscious by an explosion, it was many hours before he discovered that the Bible in his pocket had saved him from death.

(Courtesy: Mrs Sandra McAllister and Colonel Hubert K. McAllister OBE TD BDS DL)

B24 and B21 and occupy Beaucourt railway station, as well as the trenches behind the station, before taking the mill on the riverbank and two houses beyond the station. A platoon of 12th Rifles was to attack the railway sap, with another assigned to patrol the marsh. The official historian of 36th Division, Captain Cyril Falls, who served with the division, chose, strangely, to describe the action north of the Ancre as 'separate from the other and of less importance', although it was an integral part of the overall plan of advance for Fourth Army and, as noted earlier, essential to 36th Division's plan.

Cunliffe, the historian of the Royal Irish Fusiliers, describes the attack north of the Ancre as 'a bitter failure'. Although the first wave of 9th Irish Fusiliers left their trenches at 7.10am and reached the shelter of a steep ravine, in no man's land, previously reconnoitred by the battalion's Intelligence Officer, Captain Jim Menaul, those same soldiers came under heavy machine-gun fire when they rose from their positions at Zero Hour. The following waves of the battalion were cut down by machine guns as they tried to reach the ravine. This fire came not only from the front, but also from St Pierre Divion on the left flank; machine-gun posts there were able to assail the Irish Fusiliers as 29th Division's attack had been thwarted. The attackers faced at least thirteen enemy machine-gun posts, each holding a minimum of two MG 08 machine guns with a rate of fire of 300rpm and accurate at even 1,000 yards. Even so, a few men of Major T. J. Atkinson's B Company not only reached the enemy front line but broke through it and were last seen heading for Beaucourt Station. None survived. Atkinson, a 38-year-old solicitor from Portadown, was among the dead, killed in the early stages of the advance.

Edmonds' *Official History of the War* recounts how:

> A young artillery officer, who was in an observing station alongside his major, said 'Why do they stop there? Why don't they move?' 'They will never move more,' replied the more experienced officer.

The Germans were quick to restore their position on this section of the front. Of 9th Royal Irish Fusiliers there were few survivors: the 10 per cent reserve who were kept out of battle, those in battalion HQ who were not permitted to accompany the first advance, the small number of survivors who lay out in no man's land, and the few who had managed to get back to their own trenches. That evening a roll call made clear that none of the officers and only eighty soldiers were uninjured; nine officers and 235 men were dead or dying of wounds. Overall the battalion lost 535 officers and men killed, wounded or missing; it had deployed 600 into battle that morning. In 36th (Ulster) Division only 13th Rifles and 11th Inniskillings suffered more casualties, losing 595 and 589 all ranks respectively. (Thirty-two battalions suffered over 500 casualties that day.)

In his efforts to recover some of the battalion's wounded, 9th Royal Irish Fusiliers' adjutant, Lieutenant Geoffrey St George Shillington Cather earned another posthumous Victoria Cross for the Ulster Division. From 7.00pm until midnight on 1 July Lieutenant Cather searched no man's land for wounded Faughs and brought in three men. He resumed his task at 8 o'clock next morning and, under machine-gun and artillery fire, brought in another wounded man and gave water to others for whom he arranged rescue. He moved out again to take water to another man and, having done so, called out to enquire if any other wounded were about. While responding to a wave from a wounded Faugh, he was hit and killed by enemy machine-gun fire. Cather was born in London in 1890 but his mother was a Shillington from Portadown, in which town a bridge is named for the family, which also produced a chief constable of the RUC GC, while his uncle, Major David Graham Shillington, father of that eminent policeman, was a company commander in the 9th Battalion. Major Shillington's son, Thomas Graham, was also commissioned in 9th Faughs and was the assistant adjutant to his cousin.

The other battalion attacking north of the Ancre, 12th Royal Irish Rifles, had fared no better. They too had come under lethal fire from machine guns and, although pressing forward bravely, had been unable to take and hold their objectives. The first attack was beaten back but the survivors were re-formed twice by courageous officers who led them forward again on both occasions. However, they had lost their artillery support and had no means of communicating with the guns, and their efforts were in vain. Those who did reach the German trenches were unable to penetrate the line. Ballyclare man Bob Grange, serving in the signals arm of the Royal Engineers, recalled that C Company of 12th Rifles, the Ballyclare company, suffered heavily through their position on the divisional flank.

> Every time they pushed forward they were enfiladed with the heavy machine-gun fire. C Company made three charges across no man's land that morning and, of course, got wiped out. ... Ballyclare ... had over thirty killed and over a hundred wounded and, mind you, that was a packet for such a small place.

44

On the Rifles' left the leading troops of 29th Division crossed the German front-line trenches only to be caught by machine-gun fire from their rear, the result of Germans who had emerged from their dug-outs to man their weapons. Once again, the failure to mop up had proved critical. Falls wrote that:

> The attack north of the Ancre was a failure, though gallantry every whit as great as that of the battalions on the left bank was behind it.

Lee-Enfield rifle

The British infantryman's standard rifle from 1895 until the late 1950s took its name from the designer of its bolt-action system, James Paris Lee, and the location of the Royal Small Arms Factory, Enfield, in which it was made. Superseding the Lee-Metford rifle, it was the fastest bolt-action rifle in the world with a 10-round magazine; it fired a .303-inch round. For close fighting the rifle could be fitted with a Pattern 1907 sword bayonet.

British infantry fire diminished. Whereas a soldier of the Regular Army in 1914 could hit an opponent with three rounds in rapid succession in field conditions, by 1916 the best that could be hoped for was that an infantryman could shoot straight at short ranges when required. It was said that New Army soldiers spotting a German at 300 yards were more likely to throw a grenade than shoot at him.

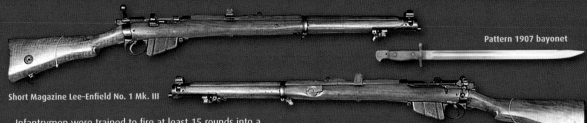

Pattern 1907 bayonet

Short Magazine Lee–Enfield No. 1 Mk. III

Infantrymen were trained to fire at least 15 rounds into a two-foot-diameter (61cm) circle in 60 seconds. Many could fire as many as 30 rounds into the target with the same degree of accuracy and the absolute record for a bolt-action rifle is still held by Sergeant-Instructor Snoxall, of the School of Musketry at Hythe, who fired 38 rounds into a one-foot-diameter (30cm) target at 300 yards (274m) in 60 seconds.

Pre-war infantrymen spent much time on musketry training (a term used until the Second World War) and it is not surprising that some German soldiers, faced with the intensive fire of British infantry battalions in 1914, believed that many of their opponents were armed with machine guns. In fact, there were only two Vickers machine guns per battalion.

The soldier who went to war in 1914 was armed with the Short Magazine Lee-Enfield (SMLE) Mark III. Complicated and expensive to manufacture (£3.75 per rifle), this was replaced by a simpler version, the SMLE Mark III*.

Large numbers of wartime recruits made it impossible to provide the same level of musketry training and the accuracy of

Plans had been made to replace the SMLE Mark III before war broke out but so many teething problems occurred with the Pattern 1913 Lee-Enfield and its .276-inch round that trials were stopped when war broke out. The British soldier, and his Commonwealth and Imperial cousins, soldiered on with the .303-inch Lee-Enfield in several variants for over four decades.

LEE ENFIELD RIFLE

Designed	1895 (SMLE 1907)
Weight	4000 g
Length	1118 mm
Barrel length	767 mm SMLE 640mm)
Ammunition	.303-inch in 10-round magazine
Production	17,000,000+

Interestingly, he also described 9th Royal Irish Fusiliers as 'one of the best [battalions] in the Division'.

That afternoon, the survivors of 12th Rifles were relieved by a battalion of York and Lancasters of 148 Brigade (from 49th Division), while two companies of York and Lancasters arrived to support 9th Royal Irish Fusiliers. By early evening the remnants of both Irish battalions had been withdrawn to Hamel village, leaving York and Lancasters holding the front. Parties of soldiers were organised to search for wounded in no man's land, a task in which 16th Rifles, the divisional pioneer battalion assisted.

Also searching no man's land was a soldier of 12th Royal Irish Rifles, who had lost his officer, and who was to be the only VC laureate of 36th (Ulster) Division on 1 and 2 July to survive to receive his Cross. Private Robert Quigg, who came from near the Giant's Causeway, had worked as a farm labourer for David Forsythe of Turfahun before obtaining employment on the Macnaghten estate. Having joined the Bushmills Company of the UVF, he enlisted in the Royal Irish Rifles and went to war as the batman (servant) for Sir Harry Macnaghten Bt, who commanded a platoon in 12th Rifles. Quigg, described as being 'about six feet in height and of powerful build', took part in three attempts to assault the German line on 1 July. Then:

> Early next morning, hearing a rumour that his platoon officer was lying out wounded, he went out seven times to look for him, under heavy shell and machine-gun fire, each time bringing back a wounded man. The last man he dragged in on a waterproof sheet from within a few yards of the enemy's wire. He was seven hours engaged in this most gallant work, and finally was so exhausted that he had to give it up.

Second Lieutenant Macnaghten's body was never found, although there was a report that he had been seen sitting in a German trench, having been wounded in both legs.

The battle for the Schwaben Redoubt continued with most of the survivors of 109 and 107 Brigades engaged. Communication was proving a major problem with landlines cut and those signallers who attempted to repair them, or to lay lines to the foremost troops, killed by machine-gun fire. That fire also cut down runners, leaving Divisional HQ and the brigade HQs unable to contact their fighting troops; there were, as yet, no wireless sets suitable for battlefield use. However, reports had been received at Divisional HQ of the failures on either flank of the Ulstermen and Nugent

46

had quickly appreciated the full nature of the threat to his men. At 8.32am he had sought permission from X Corps HQ to stop 107 Brigade's planned advance. Corps HQ had responded by saying that 107 had to advance as planned to support a new attack on Thiepval and another by VIII Corps north of the Ancre. Three-quarters of an hour later X Corps HQ had a change of heart and advised Nugent to hold 107 Brigade on its start lines until the situation to either flank had become clearer. Although that message was passed immediately to 107's commander, Brigadier General W. M. Withycombe, the latter's attempts to pass it forward to his battalions were thwarted by cut landlines and the inability of runners to get forward. Eventually, the holding order arrived, but too late: the battalions had left their start lines and were passing through the steel hail of the German defences.

Describing the ebb and flow of any battle is difficult but describing that which took place in the Schwaben Redoubt would be impossible. Fighting was confused with the soldiers of 109 and 107 Brigades enclosed in a salient, subject to German attack from their front and both flanks. They suffered also from the fog of war and the breakdown in communications. Survivors of the Derrys reported being shelled by their own artillery, but those guns were firing on target and as planned; the Derrys' speedy advance had taken them farther forward than planned, but this information could not be passed to the gunners.

It was in the horror of the fighting in the redoubt that an officer of the 9th Inniskillings earned another Victoria Cross[3] for the Ulster Division. Captain Eric Norman Frankland Bell commanded 109 Trench Mortar Battery and when the advance was:

> checked by enfilading machine-gun fire, [he] crept forward and shot the machine gunner. Later, on no less than three occasions, when our bombing parties were unable to advance, he went forward alone and threw trench mortar bombs among the enemy. When he had no more bombs available, he stood on the parapet, under intense fire, and used a rifle with great coolness and effect on the enemy advancing to counter-attack. Finally, he was killed rallying and re-organising infantry parties which had lost their officers.

Captain Bell VC has no known grave and is commemorated on the Thiepval Memorial, as are Lieutenant Cather VC and Private McFadzean

---

[3] Chronologically, this was the second VC gained by a member of the Division that day, having been preceded only by Billy McFadzean's.

VC. Born in Enniskillen, the son of an Inniskilling Fusilier, Bell was working in Liverpool when war broke out but returned to join his father's regiment and was commissioned in the Tyrones.

Bell had led his battery as far as the Crucifix, a feature believed to mark the front right corner of the Schwaben Redoubt. It was there that Captain James Proctor, commanding C Company of the Derrys, was killed. As he jumped into a trench Proctor was shot by a German officer who promptly discarded his weapon and raised his arms in surrender. Proctor's men were in no mood to accept his surrender and took swift revenge for the death of their commander. Close to the Crucifix was the last spot any sighting was made of another C Company officer, Lieutenant Ernest McClure. In the confusion of battle, McClure, with some of the company, clung on to the Derrys' position as the tide of action turned in favour of the Germans. Attempts to take ammunition and water to them were unsuccessful. Lieutenant McClure's body was never found. Although he was Mentioned in Despatches, survivors of the Derrys considered that the 32-year-old had deserved the Victoria Cross, but there were no officer witnesses to his valour and so no recommendation could be made.

Some of the Derrys made it to what was described as the German fifth line. They numbered only a few, among them being Jim Donaghy, Bobby Reid, Alfie Bogle, Alex Millar and Harry Wilson. Of those named, Private Millar was killed that day and Bogle, by then commissioned, was killed in August 1917; the others survived the war.

The Crucifix also witnessed some of the fiercest fighting for the Tyrones. Finding himself cut off, Lance Corporal Dan Lyttle, from Ardstraw, came across two abandoned machine guns, a Vickers and a Lewis. Picking up the latter, he engaged the enemy until his ammunition was finished. He then destroyed both weapons to deny them to the Germans, took up his rifle and fought his way back to his comrades, using grenades to clear the way. Another man, Private J. Gibson, reached the German wire where he saw a machine gun firing from the parapet. He attacked the trench singlehandedly and engaged the gun crew, killing all three men by using his rifle as a club. According to Canning's *A Wheen of Medals*, Sergeant S. Kelly dashed across machine-gun-swept ground several times to contact other members of the battalion on the right flank. He succeeded and subsequently took overall command, as all the officers had become

48

casualties, until wounded himself. Kelly is believed to have been one of the few to wear his Orange sash that day.

Lieutenant Henry Gallaugher, from Manorcunningham, County Donegal, distinguished himself at the Crucifix and was to earn the Distinguished Service Order, second only to the VC, that day. Advancing with A and D Companies of 11th Inniskillings, the Donegal and Fermanaghs, Gallaugher found himself the only surviving officer and, despatching a party to the C Line under Sergeant Major Stephen Bullock, took the remaining men to help consolidate the Crucifix. Having blocked the communication trenches leading to the feature and begun cutting firesteps, he returned to the A Line to bring forward men and *matériel*. There he found that the Germans had occupied part of the line, whereupon he organised a bombing party to evict them before building a barricade to which he assigned a small group of men. He also despatched a runner to report the tactical situation, but the man became disoriented by the plethora of shell holes and the smoke that shrouded the ground and delivered his message to the Tyrones. Meanwhile Gallaugher collected all the soldiers he could find in the A Line and nearby shell holes, took them forward to the Crucifix and placed his group under command of Major Peacocke, second in command of 9th Inniskillings. Lieutenant McKinley, of the Tyrones, also joined the defenders.

Peacocke had succeeded in crossing no man's land at noon and had arrived in the front line close to Point A12. There he gathered a small group of men, beat off Germans trying to bomb their way up from Thiepval and made his way to the Crucifix, taking command of the 'garrison' there. His assessment of the situation was bleak, as Falls notes:

> He speedily discovered that the holding of the ground here, now slipping from our hands, was an impossibility unless Thiepval were taken. The men were still determined, but at their last gasp from fatigue. There was scarcely any ammunition or water for the Vickers guns,[4] and it was all but impossible to send it up.

Major Blair Oliphant, second in command of 11th Rifles, also carried out 'an admirable reconnaissance' and his assessment was equally bleak. German counter-attacks included several launched from St Pierre Divion, of bitter memory, in which bombers played a major role. However, 8th and 9th Rifles, with the few men of 13th Rifles still on that

---

[4] The Vickers machine gun was water-cooled.

flank, repelled the attackers repeatedly. Among the dead of 13th Rifles was Captain James Samuel Davidson, whose father, Samuel Clement Davidson, was the inventor of air conditioning and owner of the Sirocco Works in Belfast. The 39-year-old Davidson was believed to have earned the Victoria Cross that day and Captain Wilfred Spender, of divisional HQ, in a letter to his wife, commented that he had written to Mrs Davidson of the Sirocco Works 'whose son was killed after earning the VC'. However, no VC was awarded to Davidson.

On the other flank, enemy reaction was slower. An officer of 9th Rifles, Lieutenant Sanderson, went forward to reconnoitre the trench known as Mouquet Switch on 32nd Division's front and found it unoccupied. However, it could not be pressed into use by 107 Brigade as the machine guns in Thiepval were still sweeping no man's land and few could survive their fire. Although two companies of 16th Rifles, the pioneer battalion, were sent forward to dig a communication trench along which bombs and water could have been transported, machine-gun fire also put an end to this enterprise with the 16th's commanding officer, Lieutenant Colonel John Leader, reporting, at 2.00pm, that the task was impossible.

> Supplies had run out, and the little parties that strove to bear them across were annihilated by fire. After noon attacks came upon the right flank also, the 11th Inniskillings at the Crucifix, and the 9th in the Schwaben Redoubt, being hard beset.

At this stage the French gunners were ordered to fire a flank barrage on the right, a task that was executed 'admirably', as Falls records.

As the day wore on, further German reinforcements arrived and the pressure on the attackers, who had now become the besieged, intensified. During the morning 146 Brigade of 49th Division had crossed the Ancre and, at 3.00pm, had been ordered to attack Thiepval under cover of an artillery bombardment. Once again, attackers were scourged by heavy machine-gun fire and the attack ground to a standstill. According to Falls, it was, 'in fact, stopped after the leading battalion, the 1/6th West Yorks, had seen the platoons which strove to deploy wither away.' At much the same time the Germans counter-attacked in the open on the left flank with two companies which left the cover of the trees in the Ancre valley to advance on C11. Both companies were wiped out by artillery fire and the Lewis guns of 8th Rifles as they ascended the slope.

About an hour after the abortive attack by 146 Brigade, Nugent's HQ was told that this Yorkshire brigade was at 36th Division's disposal. However, although Withycombe, the senior brigade commander in Thiepval Wood, was ordered to deploy two 146 Brigade battalions[5] to the Schwaben Redoubt, where they would reinforce and rally the Ulstermen who were being forced back, it transpired that the brigade was not yet at Nugent's 'disposal'. Two of its battalions had been committed to the failed attack on Thiepval but the other pair had followed up behind them and deployed into 32nd Division's trenches. This misunderstanding meant that it was after 7.00pm before six companies of Yorkshiremen moved up towards the C Line. By then it was too late. The unfortunate companies were moving into a situation where all was already lost. Their fate was to be beaten off by machine-gun fire from the German defenders.

To the left of 108 Brigade were deployed the units of 29th Division's 87 Brigade: 2nd South Wales Borderers, 1st King's Own Scottish Borderers, 1st Royal Inniskilling Fusiliers and 1st Border Regiment. These veterans of Gallipoli were known as the 'Incomparables' and their objective was the village of Beaumont Hamel with the Inniskillings directed on Y Ravine. The corps plan was for twin attacks to either side of the village with 4th Division advancing along the Redan Ridge to the north and 29th along Hawthorn Ridge and the deep valley – Y Ravine – to the south.

This was one of the sectors where a mine had been dug. VIII Corps' commander, Lieutenant General Hunter-Weston, wanted to explode this mine, under a German redoubt on Hawthorn Ridge, four hours before Zero. He believed that this would prompt the Germans to stand to in anticipation of an attack, but that they would then decide that no attack was about to happen and stand down, meaning that the attack at 7.30am would gain surprise. Haig turned down this request, although he agreed to the mine being detonated ten minutes before Zero. This was a major error as the mine exploding warned the Germans of imminent attack; this was compounded by Hunter-Weston's decision to lift the artillery bombardment along the line ten minutes early, which also proved tragic.

Major General de Lisle, GOC of 29th Division, launched his attack with two brigades, 86 and 87, with 88 Brigade due to follow an hour later, pass through the leading formations and go on to the final objective.

---

[5] The brigade's battalions were 1/5th, 1/6th, 1/7th (Leeds Rifles) and 1/8th (Leeds Rifles) Battalions The Prince of Wales's Own West Yorkshire Regiment.

This photograph was taken by Colonel R. D. Perceval-Maxwell of the Royal Irish Rifles and is dated 1 July 1916. It shows a wrecked German trench in the D Line. If the date is correct, this suggests that some elements of 36th (Ulster) Division had almost broken through the German first line.

Once again German machine guns decided the battle. Hardly a single man crossed the German wire, but there was some confusion as rockets rose from the German trenches and it was not clear if these were signs of British or German success. Enemy defences were terraced on a glacis 'of quarter of a mile of bare slope which the attacking infantry had to cross' which made the attackers' task impossible. The loss of the eight attacking battalions seemed so unlikely that it was some time before it was appreciated that the attack had failed completely. As a result, two battalions of 88 Brigade were ordered forward, but only one appeared immediately and was cut to pieces with the second highest casualty toll of the day: this was the Newfoundland Regiment which suffered 684 dead, wounded or missing. The Essex, delayed in the communication trenches, met a similar fate shortly afterwards when they launched their attack.

The Inniskillings' losses were grievous with 559 casualties. Their commanding officer, Lieutenant Colonel R. C. Pierce, was among the dead. The battalion war diary provides a sober summary:

> **Z Day**: In accordance with Orders the Battalion advanced on the objective, which consisted of the first three lines of German trenches, the Battalion advancing in lines of Platoons in single file on the following rotation – B, A, D Coys, C Coy being held in Reserve in our original front-line trench. Immediately our lines appeared on the parapet, the enemy brought heavy machine-gun … fire to bear which heavily decimated [sic] the advance, none being able to gain further ground than the enemy's wire. Under the circumstances the advance failed in the sector allotted to the Battalion as it was also found impossible to bring up Reserves. Strength of the Battalion on entering the Action: Officers 36; Other Ranks 916. Casualties: Officers – Lieutenant Colonel Pierce, (Temp) Captain French, Lieut Harboard and 2/Lieut Porter Killed; Missing 4; Wounded 11. Other Ranks: Killed 50; Missing 225; Wounded 265. Remainder of Battalion rallied on our [Front Sector], near St John's Road.

Also attacking in 87 Brigade were the men of 1st Royal Dublin Fusiliers who were held up behind another battalion which 'failed to attain its objective'. It was:

> eight o'clock before [two] companies began moving out over the parapets. Our own barbed wire was cut only at intervals and by this time the Germans had machine guns trained on these gaps, the result being that our casualties were very high. Only a few of our men ever got through, and fewer still succeeded in advancing more than 50 or 60 yards before being shot down.

The attack was abandoned and the survivors ordered back to their own lines. The Dubs had lost 230 officers and men.

By 10 o'clock Hunter-Weston realised that his attack had failed utterly: not a single objective had been gained and VIII Corps had suffered the highest losses of any corps in Fourth Army that day.

On the right flank of the Ulster Division was 32nd Division, to which was assigned the task of taking Thiepval village. Among the battalions in the division's 96 Brigade was 2nd Inniskillings, a unit that had been in France since August 1914. The 'Lumps', as they were known, had been transferred to 32nd Division, a New Army formation, in January 1916 and served alongside three Pals battalions in 96 Brigade, 16th Northumberland

Fusiliers and 15th and 16th Lancashire Fusiliers, the two Lancashire units being, respectively 1st and 2nd Salford Pals.

Relieved in their trenches in the Thiepval sub-sector by 15th Lancashire and 16th Northumberland Fusiliers on the night of 30 June/1 July, the Inniskillings arrived at the 'Bluff' at 3.30am to be in reserve for 96 Brigade's attack at Zero Hour. A company was deployed to 'French Street' at 8.05am while battalion HQ and two companies moved to 'Johnston's Post' at 10 o' clock. The fourth rifle company stayed at the Bluff until it was ordered to Johnston's Post at 11.30am. By this stage it was clear that the divisional plan had gone awry and, at 11.50am, two companies were ordered to attack 'well to the North to try to turn Thiepval'. This attack began at 1.00pm on a two-platoon frontage but met with intensive machine-gun fire and came to naught.

At 3.30pm 2nd Inniskillings were ordered to support the left flank of 49th Division (which was to attack at 4.00pm) and to fill the gap between that formation and 36th (Ulster) Division. It will be remembered that 49th Division was moving forward to support the Ulstermen but the planned attack on the left did not take place as only a single battalion of the 49th arrived safely, but at 4.15. As a result the Lumps occupied trenches on the right of 49th Division, remaining there until relieved by 75 Brigade of 25th Division on the evening of the 3rd. The battalion returned to 96 Brigade the following night. Figures for casualties covered the period 1-4 July and totalled 162 all ranks killed, wounded or missing, of whom ten men were listed as killed.

Five battalions of Royal Inniskilling Fusiliers took part in the first day of the Battle of Albert and together suffered over 2,000 casualties.

Eighth Division was a regular formation created in October 1914 from units called back from various parts of the Empire. Among those was the 1st Battalion Royal Irish Rifles, which had been stationed in Aden. The Rifles joined 25 Brigade with whom the battalion was serving in 1916. On Z Day the divisional objectives were Ovillers and Pozières, the latter on almost the highest point of the Thiepval plateau; the church tower in Pozières provided the Germans with an excellent artillery observation post with a clear view into the British rear lines. The division was to attack with all three brigades in line – 25 Brigade in the centre, 23 Brigade on the right and 70 Brigade on the left.

The right flank of [25 Brigade] was to be on the north of the ruined village of Ovillers. The final objective was to run through the eastern portion of Pozières. Beyond Ovillers the ground dropped away to a slight valley, rising again to Pozières.

By the end of the day 8th Division would have sustained one of the highest casualty rates in the attacking formations. With 5,121 casualties, its losses were exceeded only by 34th and 29th Divisions (6,380 and 5,240 respectively) and were marginally higher than the 5,104 of 36th (Ulster) Division. Yet the attack of 8th Division, some 8,500 bayonets, was opposed by only two battalions, about 1,800 men, of the German 180th Regiment; the boundaries of both formations were almost exactly the same. Throughout the day 180th Regiment had to call in only a single company of its reserve battalion to meet the British attack and the regiment's casualties came only to 280 men.

In 25 Brigade's attack plan the Rifles were the supporting battalion behind 2nd Royal Berkshires, on the right, and 2nd Lincolns, on the left; 2nd Rifle Brigade was the reserve battalion. Had the attack gone to plan, the Rifles would have passed through the leading battalions to its own objective. It soon became clear that the Germans held the upper hand. The leading battalions of 25 Brigade met a withering fire and the attack was paralysed. A and B Companies of 1st Rifles were moving up the communication trenches, which were being bombarded heavily by German artillery. As A Company tried to make its way along a trench, two 5.9-inch shells fell into the middle of one platoon, killing or injuring everyone. Of 121 men of the company who set out, only twenty-four completed the journey. One Rifles' officer reported that 'only two companies [got] over and no one appeared to come back'.

The companies that got over were C and D. C met very heavy fire and its platoons were wiped out before they had got very far, the wounded killed where they lay by artillery fire. The company commander, Second Lieutenant H. M. Glastonbury, suffered a leg wound in no man's land. Although his limb was bandaged, his men could not carry him back to their own lines and he perished where he lay. D Company went into action at 7.45am, forming up in columns of platoons in no man's land before advancing towards the enemy where the company broke through to the B Line and linked up with survivors of 2nd Lincolns under Lieutenant Colonel Reginald Bastard. Lieutenant S. D. I. Smith, the company commander, received a bayonet wound at the B Line but his injury did not deter him from making for the C Line, hurling grenades as he did so. Smith was then hit and killed by machine-gun fire. D Company was forced to withdraw to conform with the troops on either flank. Its riflemen had been involved heavily in close-quarter combat during the advance and withdrawal. The battalion war diary commented that:

> The German trenches had been completely buried by our bombardment but excellent use had been made of the cellars in Ovillers; his trenches were thickly manned.

Casualties in the Rifles were extremely heavy and were such that the assistant adjutant, Lieutenant Whitfield, found it impossible to produce an accurate account of the battalion's experiences, in which the commanding officer, Lieutenant Colonel Macnamara, had been wounded badly – he would succumb to his wounds on 15 July – and the adjutant killed.

Ten minutes before midnight 8th Division was withdrawn from the line.

On the left flank of 29th Division was the regular 4th Division, with two battalions from 48th Division attached. Serving in 10 Brigade of 4th Division was 1st Battalion Royal Irish Fusiliers, commanded by Lieutenant Colonel W. A. V. Findlater, who had succeeded Lieutenant Colonel Shuter on 24 May on the latter's promotion to command 109 Brigade in 36th (Ulster) Division. Under Findlater's command the battalion completed its preparations for the offensive. The Faughs were not to be committed in the first assault and reached their assembly trenches for Z Day at 12.35am on 1 July. Those trenches were on the sunken road from Auchonvillers[6] to the Sucrerie, a disused sugar factory. The march was across country using tracks indicated by white posts, a route that avoided villages that were subject to heavy German shelling, and which allowed the battalion to reach the assembly area without casualties. The Faughs were not to leave the assembly trenches until 9.30am on the 1st.

As left support battalion of 10 Brigade, the Faughs had a frontage of 375 yards and adopted a formation of three companies in the first line, with each company in company column, ninety yards between companies and 100 yards separating platoons. One company moved behind in support, using a star formation, with platoons at 200 yards distance and interval. Officers dressed 'as nearly as possible like their men' and also carried

---

[6] Known to the soldiers as Ocean Villas.

weapons and equipment like their men. Ten Brigade's role depended on the success of 11 Brigade while that of the Faughs depended on the success of the leading battalions of 10 Brigade. The divisional objectives were Ridge Redoubt and Beaumont Hamel.

As elsewhere along the front, little went according to plan. At 9.30, as the battalion began moving forward, white lights were seen in the air to the front and these were taken for the signal that objectives had been reached. That signal was a group of three white lights. Unfortunately, these were single white lights indicating 'held up by wire' and the advance was halted with the leading platoons stopped at the Tenderloin and Mountjoy trenches. At 10.25 a further message was received that 10 Brigade was not to be committed until further orders as 29th Division was not attacking Beaumont until 1.50pm.

Thus the Faughs waited for further orders whilst 'a fairly heavy artillery fire' fell around them. Just before 1.30 Colonel Findlater received an order to detach a company to reinforce 2nd Seaforth Highlanders, and some elements of 11 Brigade,[7] who were holding the Quadrilateral, a salient in the enemy line in the fork of the road junction south-west of Serre; to the Germans this fortification was the *Heidenkopf*. The Germans were attempting to force the defenders out of their positions by artillery bombardment and bombing attacks. Captain E. R. Wilson, with C Company, was ordered to undertake this task. However, C Company met such heavy machine-gun and rifle fire while trying to cross the open ground to the Quadrilateral that the advance failed. Captain Wilson was among the wounded. When Findlater learned that C Company had failed to reach the Quadrilateral he ordered D Company, under Captain G. W. N. Barefoot, to join the Seaforth. Findlater made this decision at about 4.00pm, an hour after a situation report was received stating that all attacking corps, except the British VIII Corps, had taken their objectives and that 'all efforts were to be made to support Lieutenant Colonel Hopkinson in the Quadrilateral'. Hopkinson had orders to 'hold out to the last' as the Quadrilateral was required as a pivot on which to establish a new line running through Serre, which was believed to be in British hands.

Using a circuitous route, Barefoot reached the Quadrilateral from the south with two platoons, his other two platoons having been left in a

---

[7] There were men from as many as five different battalions in the Quadrilateral.

support role in the front-line trenches. However, Barefoot soon found himself commanding the defence of the Quadrilateral. The Faughs' adjutant, Captain Carden-Roe, returned from Brigade HQ at 8.30pm with orders that D Company was 'to hold the Quadrilateral at all costs'. The Seaforth and other troops under Hopkinson were to be withdrawn, leaving Barefoot's little force alone in the German front line. During the night there were fears that D Company had been wiped out as runners failed to get through but dawn found them still resolute, having fought off many enemy bombing counter-attacks. One subaltern, Second Lieutenant Ralph Le Mare 'was said to have thrown some hundreds of bombs'. That night a Faugh sergeant, searching for wounded, heard German voices and threw a grenade in their direction. The Germans were either driven off or killed and in the morning their purpose was discovered: they had been emplacing two machine guns that could have fired directly into the British positions in the Quadrilateral. With some assistance the sergeant brought one of the machine guns back to Barefoot, having disposed of the other in a deep shell hole.

In the morning Battalion HQ made contact again with Barefoot who withdrew his men under heavy fire in good order at about 11.00am. With them D Company brought all their wounded, three prisoners and a quantity of arms and stores. Carden-Roe wrote that their return provided 'a merry interlude' and that they seemed reluctant to part with their prisoners. It transpired that the orders issued to Carden-Roe at Brigade HQ had resulted from confusion and that D Company ought to have been withdrawn with the Seaforth. Barefoot's enterprise, courage and tenacity earned him the Military Cross.

The signal lights indicating 'held up by wire' that had halted the Faughs before they could be launched into a maelstrom of machine-gun fire also told of the fate of 2nd Royal Dublin Fusiliers, the 'Old Toughs', one of the leading assault units of 10 Brigade. On the right of the extended line of attackers, the Dublins were ahead of schedule but their leading companies 'came under heavy fire at once, only a few men reaching the German position'. The war diary notes that they came under enfilade fire from machine-gun positions in Beaumont Hamel and rifle and machine-gun fire from the German A Line as well as shell fire. Although attempts were made to resume the advance, these proved fruitless as it was possible to collect only some sixty men. Of twenty-three officers and 480 men who had gone into action, fourteen officers and 311 men had become casualties.

XV Corps, under Lieutenant General Sir Henry Horne, had been re-formed in France in April 1916. On 1 July the corps included 7th, 17th and 21st Divisions and its objectives were the villages of Mametz and Fricourt. Both were well fortified, one strongpoint having 4-inch steel-plate protection. The corps achieved some of the few British successes of the day with the capture of both villages. Seventh Division, described by Falls as one of the greatest that Britain ever put into the field, was focused on Mametz and its units included 2nd Royal Irish Regiment which served in 22 Brigade from May to October 1916. On the XV Corps front no man's land was quite narrow in parts and this enabled many attackers to get into the enemy A Line without falling victim to his machine guns.

The attacking formations were 20 and 91 Brigades with 22 Brigade in their rear. When orders were received to take up a new position behind 91 Brigade, the Royal Irish moved to trenches vacated by 22nd Manchester Regiment under heavy fire. The battalion was not needed to reinforce the brigade's attack as the objective had been secured. However, A Company was sent to Mametz to consolidate a position for 21st Manchesters while D Company reinforced 22nd Manchesters to repel counter-attacks. Both companies remained in position until dawn on the 2nd when they rejoined the battalion, which was still in reserve. Casualties for the day numbered fifty, from a XV Corps total of over 8,000, mostly from machine-gun fire.

Fricourt, surrounded on the 1st, was captured on the 2nd, a day on which the Royal Irish were ordered to new positions to consolidate part of the line and to reconnoitre Mametz Wood. With this task at an end, the battalion rejoined 22 Brigade and bivouacked at Mansel Copse.

It would be unjust not to mention the Tyneside Irish, the battalions of Northumberland Fusiliers who made up 103 Brigade in 34th Division. These were 24th, 25th, 26th and 27th Northumberland Fusiliers, also known as 1st, 2nd, 3rd and 4th Tyneside Irish. Their historian notes that many of the men in the ranks had no connection with Ireland but a large proportion, some 30 per cent, were of Irish descent, in some cases the descendants of families fleeing the Great Famine, while some were native-born Irish who had come to seek work in the industrial cities and towns of north-east England. In III Corps, they fought on the left flank of 21st Division and to the right of 8th. On 1 July they attacked the cream of the Kaiser's army, the Prussian Guards, as they assailed la Boiselle on the road to Bapaume.

For the Tyneside Irish, la Boiselle was marked by:

> Ferocious personal encounters in tangled woodland [as] features of the fighting which paved the way for the later capture of Contalmaison. Their success at holding their new positions depended greatly on the progress made on their flanks. The [GOC] afterwards wrote to the Tyneside Committee: 'It is with the greatest pride and deepest regret that I inform you that Tyneside Irish covered [themselves] with glory on 1 July, but the losses were very heavy.'

So heavy were those losses that two of 103 Brigade's units, 1st and 4th Tyneside Irish, are numbered among the thirty-two battalions suffering more than 500 casualties; their losses were 620 and 539 respectively, with 1st Tyneside Irish's commanding officer among the dead and the COs of 2nd and 3rd Tyneside Irish wounded. Casualties in 34th Division were the highest of any British division that day, totalling 6,380, over 1,000 more than in the next highest formation, 29th Division.

On the southern end of Fourth Army's line, at its junction with the French Sixth Army, was disposed XIII Corps with 18th (Eastern) and 30th Divisions. Lieutenant General Walter Congreve VC's corps was the only

Troops help to push an ambulance in Mametz Wood during July. The original caption notes that the ambulance belonged to 16th (Irish) Division but, since this formation was still in the Loos sector, it may have belonged to 36th (Ulster) Division, making the date sometime during the period of heavy rain in June.

© Imperial War Museums (Q 4015)

60

one in Fourth Army to achieve all its objectives that day. Although there were no Irish units in either assaulting division, an Irish officer played a major part in the success gained by 18th Division. That officer was Major Alan Brooke, Brigade Major of 18th Division's artillery. A Francophile, Brooke had taken a French artillery officer, Colonel Herring, around 18th Division's sector in March and from him learned the details of the French 'creeping' or 'rolling' bombardment. Brooke developed the French system by producing clear maps on which the bombardment could be set out with all its timings and refinements 'on the artillery board and fire orders worked out from it'. In the weeks before Z Day, Brooke had spent much time on his system and each of the division's artillery brigades were provided with tracings that showed lanes for each battery with the exact timings of each bombardment and the 'lifts' onto the next bombardment. For his work in the Somme offensive, Brooke received the DSO. His work, combined with the superb training conducted by the GOC, Major General Ivor Maxse,[8] a Coldstreamer, ensured that 18th Division was the most successful of all British divisions that day: the first objective was taken in twenty minutes and most objectives were seized and held while its neighbouring 30th Division took and held Montauban.

Major Alan Brooke

Major Alan Brooke was the ninth child of Sir Victor Brooke Bt, of Colebrooke, County Fermanagh, and Lady Brooke, formerly Alice Bellingham. He was born near Pau in the French Pyrenees in 1883 and spoke French as his first language. The Brooke family arrived in Ireland during the Elizabethan era when they were granted land in County Donegal. An ancestor, Henry, held Donegal castle during the 1641 rebellion, for which he was rewarded with 30,000 acres in County Fermanagh, confiscated from the executed Concobhar Rua Maguire.

Commissioned in the Royal Artillery in 1902, Alan was selected for the Royal Horse Artillery before war broke out and went to France with N Battery, the Eagle Troop. Following his service with 18th (Eastern) Division, he was posted to the Canadian Corps and drafted the fireplan for the Canadian assault on Vimy Ridge in April 1917. By the end of the war he was a lieutenant colonel and GSO I (General Staff Officer) at First Army HQ.

During the Second World War he became Chief of the Imperial General Staff (CIGS) and was promoted to field marshal. As chairman of the Chiefs of Staff he was Churchill's right-hand man in the strategic direction of the war. In 1945 he was created Baron Alanbrooke of Brookeborough and Viscount Alanbrooke in 1946. From 1949 until his death in June 1963 he was Chancellor of Queen's University, Belfast.

Five Irish cavalry regiments were awarded the 'Somme 1916' battle honour: 4th (Royal Irish) Dragoon Guards, 6th (Inniskilling) Dragoons, 8th (The King's Royal) Irish Hussars, the North Irish Horse and the South Irish Horse. In the first named there were few Irishmen, even though the regiment was nicknamed the 'Mounted Micks'; in 1914, from a total of 561 all ranks, only thirty-nine were Irish. As with other cavalry regiments, during the lengthy period of trench warfare they spent much of their time waiting for the breakthrough that would lead to a breakout in which cavalry would come into their own. At other times cavalry regiments were 'dismounted' with their men serving in the trenches as infantry. In spite of the 'Somme 1916' battle honour, the campaign is not mentioned in the Inniskillings' regimental history; in the course of the war the Inniskillings' losses totalled 185 all ranks. The Irish Hussars were in the Ambala Cavalry Brigade of 1st Indian Cavalry Division and had but a peripheral role at the Somme.

The two Irish reserve cavalry regiments, North Irish Horse and South Irish Horse, were more involved. As already noted, 1st North Irish Horse had a role in Third Army's diversionary operation at Gommecourt although mostly deployed on VII Corps administrative tasks, such as traffic control, rather than receiving and guarding German prisoners which had been their planned employment. Similarly, 2nd North Irish Horse, in X Corps, were probably deployed to similar administrative tasks, but no war diary was maintained for the first three days of July. In XV Corps, the South Irish Horse were employed as the corps cavalry regiment, a role filled by two squadrons of the regiment and the Wiltshire Yeomanry.

---

8 Maxse was later appointed to oversee all training in the BEF.

5 The Battle Continues: Albert to Bazentin

The Battle of the Somme did not end with the setting of the sun on 1 July 1916. It would rage for all of that month, the three following months, and into November. For 36th (Ulster) Division, however, its engagement on the Somme lasted only that day, although parties of soldiers continued to search for wounded on the 2nd when the relief of the division by 49th Division was completed. The days that followed were bitter ones for the officers and men of the Ulster Division. Private Harry Bennett was one of the Derrys who paraded in Martinsart Wood for a roll call. The battalion was over 400 fewer in number than it had been at Zero Hour the previous day. Bennett, an orderly at battalion HQ, had been one of those kept back and was never able to forget that roll call.

> A name would be called and someone would answer, 'He's dead', then another name and the same answer. One of the men who died was Sergeant Porter, 'Fadeaway' Porter [as] we called him. He was a great bloke, very popular. I lost a lot of friends that day.

Thomas Gibson, another 10th Inniskilling, was ill in hospital and could hardly believe the number of casualties who were brought in. His own D Company had suffered especially badly.

On 5 July the Ulster Division moved back to Rubempré and eventually entrained for Flanders where they would join General Plumer's Second Army. Their next major operation would be the attack on Messines Ridge on 7 June 1917.

For Rawlinson's Fourth Army the battle continued on the Somme front. However, against Foch's wishes, Haig decided to close down the northern part of Fourth Army's line, from the Albert-Bapaume road to Gommecourt, and concentrate on the southern sector where his right wing – XV and

XIII Corps – had achieved significant success, inflicting heavy defeat on the German Second Army. In what is now defined as the first phase of the Somme campaign, 1 to 17 July, there were two battles, the first being Albert (1-13 July) and the second Bazentin Ridge (14th-17th). Battle honours were awarded for both; eight Irish regiments, including the North Irish and South Irish Horse, received the former and three the latter.

La Boisselle, where the Tyneside Irish had suffered so much on Zero Day, still held out although 19th Division had taken part of it. By the 5th the village was in British hands and inroads had been made elsewhere in the sector. Plans were made to extend those gains with 74 Brigade, detached to 12th Division from 25th Division, deployed on this task. The brigade, including 2nd Royal Irish Rifles, was to attack from la Boisselle[9] towards the eastern side of Ovillers, an almost northerly manoeuvre.

The attack began on the morning of 7 July with 9th Loyals and 13th Cheshires the leading battalions of 74 Brigade. As those units advanced the Rifles occupied the assembly trenches, with two companies behind each attacking battalion. With the Loyals and Cheshires taking their objective, the Rifles moved up and took over the captured line, suffering 167 casualties in so doing, including thirty killed. This line was held throughout the 8th until, that evening, the battalion advanced again, behind a company of Lancashire Fusiliers, and secured their objective, although consolidation took all night.

With daylight came the realisation that the battalion had advanced too far, leaving them without friendly troops to either flank. Worse still, their own artillery believed the Rifles' positions to be held by the Germans and bombarded them throughout the day, causing over forty casualties. At 4.00pm the Germans launched a two-pronged attack from Contalmaison Wood, outflanking the Rifles and forcing them to retire to their original objective, held by Lancashires and North Staffords. In spite of the ferocity of the German attack, the withdrawal was completed in good order but, by the end of that day, casualties had increased to more than a hundred, of whom thirteen had been killed. Early next morning 2nd Rifles were relieved and marched off to Senlis.

---

[9] Strictly, this village is Ovillers la Boisselle, but it was referred to as la Boisselle by the BEF to distinguish it from Ovillers which lay to the north across the Albert-Bapaume road.

64

A water-cooled Vickers machine gun crew wearing anti-gas masks near Ovillers in July 1916. The team typically comprised six to eight men.

They were back in the line, at Ovillers, on the 15th, marching 'in full daylight from Albert, now no longer shelled'. Their chaplain, Father Henry Gill SJ,[10] noted that 'We now felt that we had got into the German lines, which had seemed so impregnable, but not very far!' German troops were still holding out in the south-east corner of the village and attempts to evict them were rebuffed by intensive machine-gun fire. On 16 July, at 1.00am, a battalion attack, reinforced by two Cheshire companies, reached the foremost enemy line but 'very heavy machine-gun fire' from the front and their right flank forced an abandonment of the attack.

Pictorial Press/Alamy

[10] Born in 1872, Father Gill was Mentioned in Despatches, earned the MC and was appointed DSO, a remarkable record for a man in his 40s.

Sporadic attacks were made by bombing parties on a German bombing post, which eventually succeeded in taking it and capturing almost 130 of the Prussian 15th Regiment, including two officers. This success permitted 2nd Rifles to secure the south-eastern perimeter of Ovillers and to link their right flank to 5th Royal Warwicks. The day's fighting left six dead with over fifty wounded or missing.

This battle at Ovillers on 16 July is typical of many smaller actions fought during the Somme campaign. As part of the first phase of the Somme campaign, it earned the battle honour Bazentin for the Royal Irish Rifles, an honour shared with 2nd Royal Irish Regiment whose C Company, under Captain J. P. Tighe, had taken Bazentin-le-Petit together with 150 prisoners, including the HQ of 16th Bavarian Regiment. The Royal Irish fought off a German counter-attack, an action in which Captain T. A. Lowe distinguished himself, as did several others, including Captain E. Hegarty, CSM E. Power and Corporal Corrigan. This action drew special praise from Rawlinson who visited the Royal Irish to congratulate them. Also awarded the Bazentin battle honour were the Inniskillings and the Munsters. The Lumps had extended the British position at Ovillers on 9 and 10 July while 2nd Munsters attacked alongside 1st Glosters north of Montauban on the night of the 16th/17th, the effect of the bayonet-wielding attackers prompting the Germans to flee 'in confusion'. A position midway between Bazentin-le-Petit Wood and Pozières was seized and consolidated. Before the attack the Munsters' RSM, WO I John Ring, had asked the commanding officer if the CSMs could take part in the attack. Lieutenant Colonel W. B. Lyons agreed to two, chosen by tossing coins, doing so, and also advanced at the head of his men, earning himself a rebuke from his brigade commander. To that rebuke Lyons replied, 'Yes, Sir. I quite understand. But … what is my miserable little life as compared with those of my eight hundred brave Irishmen?' Lyons was killed a few days later while carrying out a reconnaissance.

The success of the Royal Irish at Bazentin gave Fourth Army control of five miles of the German second position, but not all objectives had been taken. In particular, High Wood and Delville Wood remained in enemy hands. Even so, an attempt was made to launch a cavalry attack but although units of 2nd Indian Cavalry Division were sent forward there was no breakout and the regiments had to fight dismounted.

6 The Second Phase: Fromelles to Ginchy

The second phase of the campaign began on 19 July with the two-day Battle of Fromelles, launched by XI Corps, which included 61st Division and 5th Australian Division. Neither formation was well prepared, having arrived in France only recently; that lack of preparation contributed to the failure of this diversionary operation. No Irish units were involved, although Irishmen fought in the ranks of the Australian brigades, which lost heavily (their losses were the second worst suffered by Australian troops in any 24-hour period on the Western Front, exceeded only by Bullecourt in 1917). In the subsequent battle for the Pozières ridge, Australian soldiers also took part with 2nd Division capturing the heights on 6 August before being relieved by 4th Division, which had orders to continue the advance northwards towards Mouquet Farm. From the 11th fighting raged around the farm for four days, during which Irish-born Private Martin O'Meara, a stretcher bearer, ventured into no man's land time after time to bring in wounded. He did so even under the weight of heavy bombardments and, at least four times, brought forward water and supplies and took back wounded men. O'Meara even volunteered to carry bombs and ammunition to a section of trench that was under fierce attack. Although wounded, he persisted in his duties, showing 'utter contempt of danger', for which he was awarded the Victoria Cross.

The battle for Delville Wood (bois d'Elville) had begun on 14 July and lasted until 5 September. This series of costly engagements finally left Fourth Army holding the wood, part of the triangle of Bazentin-le-Petit Wood, High Wood and Delville Wood. The South African Brigade in 9th (Scottish) Division played a major role and suffered very heavy casualties. Of the Irish regiments only the Royal Irish and the Leinster were involved in the battle, the former's part following on from their actions at Bazentin Ridge. The Leinsters were called forward from a brigade support role on 31 August when a major German counter-attack, with air support, secured ground north of Longueval. As they marched to the line their pipers played at the front of the battalion which brought the Irish Guards 'out of their billets at Durnancourt' to show their appreciation in true Irish style. In the fighting that followed, the same officer recorded how, on more than one occasion a lone figure could be glimpsed through the smoke as he hurled grenades into an advanced German post. However, 'the bomber fell to an invisible foe … and so this unknown Irish warrior of a daring exploit was swallowed up in the weeping countryside of tortured Picardy'.

In late August 16th (Irish) Division was transferred to the Somme front. As they made their way to their new operational area, this warrant officer was photographed by a wheatsheaf as his unit made a stop for a meal.

The final battles of the second phase followed in early-September and involved all the Irish line infantry regiments. These were the battles of Guillemont (3-6 September) and Ginchy (9 September) in which 16th (Irish) Division played a major role. The initial operation had not included the Irish Division, which was held in XIV Corps reserve, but when two brigades of 20th (Light) Division sustained heavy casualties in an attack on the southern part of Guillemont, 47 Brigade, consisting of 6th Royal Irish, 6th Connaught Rangers, 7th Leinsters and 8th Royal Munster Fusiliers, was brought forward to take the northern part of the village; the brigade had been attached to 20th Division on 1 September. Although their traditional recruiting areas were in the south or in Connacht, both 6th Royal Irish and 6th Connaught Rangers had strong representation from the Ulster counties, the former including B Company, commanded by Major Willie Redmond MP, raised in Londonderry mainly from Home Rule supporters, and the latter including a large number of volunteers from west Belfast. While B Company of 6th Royal Irish mustered about 200 men from the Maiden City, about three times that

Some of the soldiers of 16th (Irish) Division were also photographed as they enjoyed the same meal break among the wheatsheaves.

number from West Belfast enlisted in 6th Connaught Rangers, although some were transferred later to 7th Leinsters.

Popular belief portrays 16th (Irish) Division as the nationalist/Catholic mirror image of 36th (Ulster) Division, but this is far from true. Even though the first GOC, Lieutenant General Sir Lawrence Parsons, claimed that the vast majority of men in 49 Brigade were Catholic, the division was never either exclusively nationalist or Catholic. In fact, 49 Brigade included four battalions from Ulster and was often referred to as the Ulster Brigade. Those four battalions were 7th and 8th Royal Inniskilling Fusiliers and 7th and 8th Princess Victoria's (Royal Irish Fusiliers). An analysis of the dead of the original Inniskilling battalions – between their raising and 31 December 1916 – shows that many were Protestant. Of the 220 dead of 7th Inniskillings in that period, 167 were born in Ireland, sixty-seven of whom were 'presumed Protestants'. The proportion of 'presumed Protestants' in 8th Inniskillings was higher still, since of the 185 dead of the period 146 were Irish-born, of whom sixty-one were Protestant. Of those 128 'presumed Protestant' soldiers of the two Inniskilling battalions, it appears that thirty-nine signed the Ulster Covenant in 1912.

As 47 Brigade went into action on 3 September its soldiers found the ground over which they were to fight 'a chaotic wilderness of shell-holes, rim overlapping rim; and, in the bottom of many, the bodies of the dead'. The village of Guillemont had disappeared in the storm of war.

One officer of 7th Leinsters noted that a pile of twenty howitzer shells lay about with the bodies of the carrying party who had been caught in British artillery fire while a large howitzer, struck by a British shell, had been overturned; and all around lay the detritus of battle – weapons, equipment and rations, as well as the tragic bodies of the fallen.

British artillery began shelling the enemy positions at Guillemont at 8.15am on the 3rd. The German guns retaliated and the waiting soldiers came under fire, exacerbated by some of their own guns and trench mortars firing short. In 6th Connaught Rangers, on the right flank of 47 Brigade, some 200 men of C and D Companies were killed or wounded by shellfire before the battalion even left its start line. The equivalent of a company had been lost, prompting the commanding officer, Lieutenant Colonel J. S. M. 'Jack' Lenox-Conyngham, from Moneymore in County Londonderry, to call forward both support companies, B and A, to reinforce the pair on the start line; this was only five minutes before Zero Hour, which was noon. As the battalion waited for Zero Hour, the CO held an O Group (orders group) for his officers. During this final briefing, a shell hit the door of the HQ dug-out and one officer, Lieutenant O'Sullivan, saw his notes covered by the blood and brains of one of his fellow officers, who had taken the brunt of the blast. A casualty being treated by the battalion's Medical Officer (MO) was blown to pieces by a shell, sending the MO into shock. In spite of all this, O'Sullivan noted that the Rangers' morale held up, aided no doubt by Lenox-Conyngham strolling about amongst the men, chatting amiably to them and reminding them that this was the day they had been waiting for since beginning their training. Even soldiers who were employed in the rear echelon in comparative safety came forward to join in the assault.

At Zero Hour the guns were to fire an intensive 3-minute bombardment, while Stokes mortar batteries poured out a rain of bombs, and aircraft assailed the enemy positions before the infantry attacked. The Connaughts were to attack towards the Quarries, along the northern side of 'Mount Street', while the Leinsters, assembled since 4.00am in the 'gridiron', specially constructed shallow trenches, were to attack south from the railway station.

Jumping off just before Zero+3, the Connaughts took the Germans by surprise and Edmonds comments on the charge of the 'impetuous Irishmen' as they surged forward. *The Daily Chronicle's* correspondent wrote of the charge through Guillemont as 'one of the most astonishing feats of the war', adding that it was 'almost too fast in its impetuosity' and 'a wild and irresistible assault'. The reporter may have been referring to the popular image of Irish infantry and to the reputation of the Connaught Rangers in particular with this purple prose. Of the Rangers, dubbed the Devil's Own in the Peninsular War, it had been said that if they could not take a position by assault they would steal it stone by stone. Lieutenant O'Sullivan saw a more orderly advance, with the platoons moving neatly until their waves were broken by shell holes after which the advance took on the appearance of a crowd invading a football pitch at the end of a match.

The Connaughts' attack was successful and all their objectives as far as 'North Street' were taken. But the price had been high with the battalion reduced to fewer than 400 all ranks, many having been killed by machine-gun fire from the Quarries. Among the dead was the CO. Jack Lenox-Conyngham was killed leading his battalion as it left its start line. The *Freeman's Journal* recorded a Connaughts' NCO tribute:

> The position we had to carry was bristling with machine guns. They sent bullets at us in shovelfuls, it seemed. Our commander stepped out and pointed to the position with his cane. 'That, Connaught Rangers, is what you have got to take,' was all he said. We said nothing for reply, but we looked enough to satisfy him we would do all that was expected of us.

The 54-year-old had been a popular and inspiring leader and his death was a matter of real regret to his men, whom he had commanded since the raising of 6th Rangers in 1914.

Lieutenant O'Sullivan was wounded in front of an intact German strongpoint but rose to his feet and followed his men to take the surrender of a number of Germans. He was hardly prepared for the numbers of enemy dead in the ruins of the village, recording that he had to step over them because he could not walk round them.

With all four companies attacking, the Rangers met with success, the enemy on the left surrendering at once, although this was when heavy casualties were incurred from the machine guns at the Quarries. On the right there was some stiffer opposition which was soon overcome and the Rangers then began clearing the cellars in the Quarries area. The first objective had been gained at 12.09pm. Eleven minutes later the second had fallen and the third, North Street, was secure at 12.55pm.

The battalion had also gained its first Victoria Cross. Private Thomas Hughes, from Coravoo, near Castleblayney in County Monaghan, was wounded in the attack but, having had his injuries dressed by a medical orderly, returned to the fray. During the subsequent fighting the 31-year old spotted a German machine gun and dashed out in front of his company to single-handedly capture the position, killing the gunner and taking the other crew members prisoner. In the course of this he had received two more wounds. Thomas Hughes survived the wounds and the war. Later promoted corporal, he received his VC from King George V in London in June 1917.

The Leinsters, too, had achieved success and a Victoria Cross. Their 'dashing assault delivered south-eastward … from the trenches beyond Guillemont Station had carried all before it.' Lieutenant John Vincent Holland, who commanded 7th Leinsters' bombers, led his twenty-six bombers in a dash forward through the British fire to surprise the Germans in their dug-outs. They ignored the fire that fell around them as they wrought havoc in the enemy lines and, by the end of the day, were reduced to five men and Lieutenant Holland but had destroyed many German bunkers, cleared a large part of the village and taken fifty prisoners. For his actions, Holland, from County Kildare, was awarded the Victoria Cross. He later served in the Indian Army before settling in Australia.[11]

Behind the Connaughts and the Leinsters came 6th Royal Irish and 8th Munsters who passed through the leading battalions to take the final objective, known as Sunken Road. In this phase of the attack the Royal Irish and Munsters were reinforced unofficially by about 140 Connaught Rangers 'whose ardour could not be restrained'. Both the Royal Irish – who had gone 'over the parapet with their pipes playing', made their advance in good order and had taken their objective to the strains of the pipes – and the Munsters fought off German counter-attacks that were delivered with vigour. (In early-July German commanders had forbidden any voluntary withdrawal by formation commanders and had decreed that any position lost should be counter-attacked immediately.)

Although 6th Connaughts were to be relieved that night, the handover was postponed as 8th Munsters on their left flank came under determined counter-attack by the Germans during the night. Since 7th Division,

---

[11] His elder son, Captain Niall Vincent Holland MC, was killed while serving in the Indian Army near Imphal in the Second World War.

on 47 Brigade's left, had failed to take Ginchy, the Munsters' left flank was exposed. On three occasions German attacks, preceded by artillery fire, were repelled and the battalion was relieved at 2.00am on the 4th by 12th King's Royal Rifle Corps and 12th Rifle Brigade. The Connaughts were not relieved until 3.50am on the 5th. Casualties had been heavy in the brigade: over 1,000 had been killed, wounded or were missing; the Rangers could muster only 194 men, although a reinforcement draft of ninety-one men arrived on the 5th; losses in 6th Royal Irish totalled 325.

Guillemont had been taken, one of only two gains that day. Wounded Germans took back the message 'The English are in Guillemont', surely not a report that would have pleased the men of 47 Brigade.

In his book *A History of the Great War*, the historian and novelist John Buchan, later Lord Tweedsmuir, wrote:

> As the bloody angle south of Beaumont-Hamel will be for ever associated with the Ulster Division, so Guillemont was a triumph for the troops of Southern [sic] Ireland. The men of Munster, Leinster and Connaught broke through the intricate defences of the enemy as a torrent sweeps down rubble. The place was one of the strongest of all the many fortified villages in the German line and its capture was the most important achievement of the British since the taking of Pozières. It was the last uncaptured point in the old German position between Mouquet Farm and the junction with the French.

Soldiers of 16th (Irish) Division return from Guillemont, having captured the village.

© Imperial War Museums (Q 4199)

Buchan seemed unaware that Guillemont was a triumph for men from all four provinces, with Ulster represented strongly within the ranks of 47 Brigade and with Ulstermen in all the brigades.

Next day 48 Brigade – 7th Rifles, 1st Royal Munster Fusiliers, 8th and 9th Royal Dublin Fusiliers – and two battalions from 49 Brigade, 7th and 8th Royal Irish Fusiliers, were detached from 16th (Irish) Division to reinforce a further attack on the Leuze Wood line by 5th Division. On the morning of 5 September the advance by 5th Division held the promise of reaching the final objective, the Combles Trench. With 16th Royal Warwicks 'within a few hundred yards of the trench', 7th Faughs were ordered to relieve the Warwicks and attack the Combles position at 4.00pm. The battalion complied with the order and moved off as planned. However, the intervening ground was not as straightforward as might have appeared. Waist-high standing corn hid belts of coiled barbed-wire defences and, as the Faughs struggled with the wire in their efforts to reach their objective, enemy machine guns opened fire and they were pinned down. At 7.30pm a further attempt was made to reach the Combles Trench but was also brought to a standstill by machine-gun fire. With 245 casualties the Faughs were relieved during the night.

German soldiers captured at Guillemont are marched back to the British lines. Watching them are gunners of the Royal Artillery.

© Imperial War Museums (Q 4172)

The following morning, the 6th, the Faughs' 8th Battalion, which had come into the line on the left, advanced across the Combles-Ginchy road. On the right A and D Companies pushed into Bouleaux Wood, an arm of Leuze Wood, although the overall tactical situation was unclear. It was soon found that both flanks were exposed, or 'in the air', and the Faughs could make no further advance. The battalion held its position until relief came in the evening, although some ground had to be given up to a counter-attack just before that relief.

A pause in operations for the Irish brigades followed. The two Inniskilling battalions of 49 Brigade arrived and command of them passed from 20th Division to HQ 16th (Irish) Division. Major General William Hickie would now control all three of his brigades in the forthcoming battle for Ginchy. Meanwhile, 2nd Royal Irish had been involved in 22 Brigade's attack towards Ginchy, although it had been the reserve unit in the initial attack, made by 20th Manchesters and 1st Royal Welsh Fusiliers with 2nd Royal Warwicks in support. The attack met with success, the Manchesters capturing the village and the Welsh taking Beer Trench. However, the Manchesters came under heavy machine-gun fire and the Welsh were pinned down at Beer Trench and so B Company of 2nd Royal Irish was ordered forward to be ready, at 3.00pm, to extend a line of four strong posts on Ginchy ridge. As Captain W. L. Moore-Brabazon's company moved up, No.8 Platoon was lost and he asked battalion HQ for reinforcements. At much the same time, the Warwicks and Manchesters were under attack and the Royal Irish were asked to lend some support; neither English battalion had any officers left.

An advanced dressing station (ADS) of the Royal Army Medical Corps (RAMC) on the Montauban-Guillemont road during the September battles. This ADS has often been identified as being with 16th (Irish) Division due to the apparent presence of shamrock symbols on the two lorries to the left but the division normally used the symbol LP, the initials of its first GOC, Sir Lawrence Parsons, on its vehicles.

© Imperial War Museums (Q 4246)

Royal Irish officers and men lent support to the Warwicks and Manchesters, Lieutenant Royall rallying a party of the latter and leading a charge on the enemy during which he was killed. Company Sergeant Major Power MC took the survivors, about six men, back to the ridge facing Ginchy where he found a small party of Warwicks in a trench and decided to hold on there until reinforcements could arrive. As other men of the Manchesters came back in confusion, Moore-Brabazon rallied them but was unable to advance to Ginchy since he had so few men and faced such doughty opposition; he had been wounded in the meantime. More confusion followed and it was discovered that the Germans had recaptured Ginchy but that some Manchesters were holding a trench near the village. The disappearance of No.8 Platoon was also explained: it had been cut off from B Company when some 400 German prisoners doubled across its front near Folly Trench, many of them jumping into the trench to avoid shellfire. Captain Considine, the platoon commander, was able to retrieve the situation and cleared Stout Trench, having obtained ammunition from a party of 6th Royal Irish, who were carrying it to Guillemont.

In spite of the best efforts of the Royal Irish the attack had ground to a standstill. The battalion was deployed by companies along the brigade front and the level of confusion may be gauged from the fact that it was discovered that the location marked on maps as Waterlot Farm was really the Sucrerie. Although the battle continued, 2nd Royal Irish could not advance beyond Stout and Porter Trenches, west of Ginchy. Other elements of XV Corps were also still engaged north-east of Delville Wood. The task of taking Ginchy now passed to 16th (Irish) Division, part of XIV Corps.

Although 16th (Irish) Division had not taken part in the earlier battles in the Somme sector, it did not arrive in Fourth Army and XIV Corps as a fresh formation. Guillemont and Ginchy may have been its first major engagements but Hickie's men had already been involved in arduous service at Loos and had sustained heavy losses in the steady attritional warfare in that sector, especially in the raiding which had been carried out by its soldiers. From January to 31 May casualties totalled 3,491, of whom 741 had been killed, while in June, July and August, the months in which they had been engaged in raiding, a further 2,670 casualties had been sustained, including 380 dead. Such had been the losses in 9th Munsters that the battalion had been disbanded on 30 May and its place in the division taken by 1st Munsters. Since 1 January 6th Royal Irish had

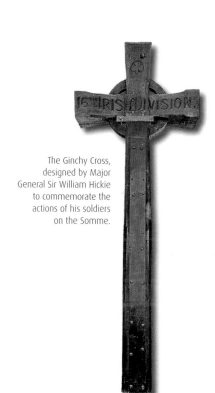

The Ginchy Cross, designed by Major General Sir William Hickie to commemorate the actions of his soldiers on the Somme.

suffered over 400 casualties, almost half its strength, while 6th Connaught Rangers had lost about a third of its strength from 1 May to 31 August.

Having been transferred from the Loos sector to the Somme, the division was thrown into action without any opportunity for rest, nor was it allowed time to familiarise its soldiers with the ground. There was no training over ground similar to that on which the battalions would fight. Instead, the brigades were deployed piecemeal into the Somme fighting.

Hickie was to carry out the operation to secure Ginchy with a much-weakened division. Since arriving in the sector, his brigades had been fighting continuously for six days, had suffered heavy losses and were

Major General Sir William Hickie

Major General Sir William Hickie, the eldest of the eight children of Colonel James Francis Hickie and Larios y Tashara, of Castile in Spain, came from a well-known military family. Educated at Oscott College, Birmingham, he entered the Royal Military College, Sandhurst, and was commissioned in his father's regiment, the Royal Fusiliers (City of London Regiment), in 1885.

Hickie served in a variety of postings from Gibraltar to India before attending Staff College as a captain. During the Second Boer War he held a number of appointments, including an independent all-arms column; he also commanded mounted infantry. He distinguished himself at the Battle of Bothaville in 1900.

There followed staff appointments and a period in Ireland, during which Hickie commanded 1st Royal Fusiliers. From 1909 to 1912 he was on the staff of 8th Division in Cork before becoming Quartermaster General, Irish Command, at the Royal Hospital, Kilmainham, in which post he helped prepare Irish Command for the forthcoming war with Germany. In 1912 he was appointed a Companion of the Order of the Bath (CB).

When war broke out Irish Command provided the staff of II Corps and moved to France with the Expeditionary Force where

Brigadier General Hickie took charge of the Adjutant and Quartermaster General's Department during the retreat from Mons. In September he assumed command of 13 Brigade in battle, before commanding 53 Brigade until December 1915 when he was recalled to England to become GOC of 16th (Irish) Division in succession to Lieutenant General Sir Lawrence Parsons.

Hickie took the division to France, having trained it to a high pitch and made major changes amongst the senior officers. He remained as GOC until falling ill in February 1918. During his tenure the division earned an outstanding reputation for its ability, the offensive nature of its soldiers and its development of operational techniques. Although not given a new command until the war was over he had proved himself one of the BEF's best divisional commanders. Hickie designed the Ginchy Cross, now in the Memorial Gardens at Islandbridge, Dublin, to commemorate the actions of his soldiers on the Somme.

Knighted in 1918, Hickie retired from the Army in 1922 and later became a Senator in the *Seanad* of the Irish Free State. As President of the British Legion in the Free State, he played a major role in promoting the welfare of ex-servicemen in Ireland. He died in November 1950.

physically and psychologically tired. Brigadier General Ramsay, commanding 48 Brigade, reported that his soldiers were so tired that, as soon as the battle for Ginchy was over, they should be relieved forthwith. In numbers all three brigades were lacking severely: 47 Brigade's four battalions averaged only 260 men each; two companies of the divisional pioneer battalion, 11th Hampshires, added another 200 men while 47 Machine Gun Company contributed a further ninety, but the entire brigade mustered little more than the strength of a full battalion. On 8 September 47 and 48 Brigades held the divisional front with 49 Brigade in reserve (its two Inniskilling battalions had lost 426 all ranks). With the ground in front of Ginchy under heavy sustained artillery bombardment, Hickie ordered his brigades to advance their inner flanks across a spur close to the railway, to do which 49 Brigade swung its left from the Guillemont-Leuze Wood road to face north-east.

Z Day for the attack on Ginchy was 9 September. On the left of XIV Corps, 47 Brigade obeyed the order to wait two minutes after Zero Hour, 4.45pm, before launching their attack. This was to allow a final intensive bombardment on the enemy's forward positions. However, 48 Brigade did not allow this interval and moved off promptly, to be met by heavy fire from the German artillery. When 47 Brigade moved off its battalions ran into machine-gun fire at close range. Leading the brigade's attack were 6th Royal Irish and 8th Royal Munsters who found the enemy 'well prepared and their trenches unharmed by our bombardment'. On the parapet of the Royal Irish objective five machine guns 'caused a decided check' and the trench could not be taken in spite of further attempts. Casualties were heavy, with the commanding officer, Lieutenant Colonel F. E. P. Curzon, among the forty-three dead while 110 were wounded and another forty missing.

The Munsters' experience was similar and, although some penetrated the enemy trench, the majority were stopped about 100 yards from their objective. Casualties were not as high as those in the Royal Irish, but almost eighty were killed or wounded. A 47 Brigade report commented that:

> From a tactical point of view nothing could have been worse for launching an attack, the Munsters had two companies in a front trench where two men could not pass without exposing themselves to machine guns and snipers, the trenches being 4 feet 6 inches to 5 feet deep. The remaining companies were in two similar and even shallower trenches, broken up in places by incessant shell fire.

Neither the Rangers nor the Leinsters, following up behind their comrades, could make any headway. For the Leinsters this day was to be the 'most disastrous … in the history of the 7th Battalion' while 7th Inniskillings, of 49 Brigade, who had tried to support 47 Brigade, found themselves countered by sustained machine-gun and rifle fire and it seemed as if the battalion might be wiped out. In 6th Connaught Rangers there were ninety-two casualties from 266 men while the brigade as a whole suffered 448 casualties with 7th Inniskillings, who had deployed in their support, losing almost 200. Next morning both the Royal Irish and the Munsters were relieved by 4th Grenadier Guards.

However, the Germans had not stopped all the attackers and, as the *Official History* records, 'Other Irishmen were now streaming into Ginchy'. These were the leading battalions of 48 Brigade which had made great progress and achieved success. Also much understrength before they started, the leading battalions – 1st Royal Munsters on the right and 7th Rifles on the left – sustained considerable losses from artillery bombardment before leaving their start lines, including from British guns whose commanders had not been told that the Irish units were forward of their own front trenches. The machine guns that had caused such suffering in 47 Brigade also targeted 48 Brigade's leading companies but the losses were less than they might have been since the Munsters' right company commander ordered his men to wheel to the

right and take up positions in a sunken road north of the railway line. A similar tactic was employed by the left company, commanded by the company sergeant major; they swung to the right and tried to continue the attack. However, little progress could be made; only one Munsters' company commander was still on his feet after fifty yards.

It was a different story for the Rifles who met only 'slight opposition'. Since the battalion had suffered heavily from shellfire while waiting for Zero Hour and only 150 men, less than a company, were left standing, 7th Royal Irish Fusiliers of 49 Brigade were ordered forward from divisional reserve to reinforce them. Both battalions attacked together, although in truth they mustered fewer men than a single full-strength battalion, and made for the German front line. Each man carried his rifle, two bandoliers of ammunition, two grenades, two empty sandbags and his iron rations,[13] a heavy weight to bear, but everything was essential. One Irish Fusiliers' subaltern recorded his memories of the attack:

> We couldn't run. We advanced at a steady walking pace, stumbling here and there, but going ever onward and upward …. I have a most vivid recollection of seeing a tremendous burst of clay and earth go shooting up into the air – yes, and even parts of human bodies – and that when the smoke cleared away there was nothing left. I shall never forget that horrifying spectacle as long as I live, but I shall remember it as a sight only, for I can associate no sound with it …. I remember men crawling about and coughing up blood, as they searched round for some place in which they could shelter …. By this time all units were mixed up, but they were all Irishmen.

Infantry advance up the slope towards Ginchy into the bombardment.
© Imperial War Museums (Q 1306)

[13] The iron ration included army biscuits (twice-baked, hence *bis-cuit*, bread) and bully beef.

The Rifles and Faughs took only minutes to reach the enemy front line. Although the Germans made a brief stand on the outskirts of Ginchy their dispositions were shattered by the attentions of 48 Trench Mortar Battery. With the German defences cracked open, the two follow-up battalions, 8th and 9th Royal Dublin Fusiliers, passed through to advance on the village itself. Such was the impetus of the Dublins' advance that a number of soldiers passed right through the village and some distance beyond. However, since they could not be supported they were pulled back to Ginchy where 48 Brigade consolidated its gains. Lieutenant Colonel Sir Edward Bellingham, commanding 8th Dublins, informed Sir Lawrence Parsons, the division's first GOC, of their success, commenting that 'We were left in the air on both flanks, which made our exploit all the more praiseworthy'. Bellingham had captured fourteen Germans himself, from a brigade 'bag' of 200. A large number of those prisoners were Bavarians who were happy to be captured by Irishmen they presumed to be Catholics like themselves. They soon made themselves known to 16th Division's Catholic chaplains.

But the battle was not over. On 48 Brigade's left flank 55th Division had failed to secure its objectives. Together with 47 Brigade's failure on the right this meant that 48 Brigade held a salient around Ginchy. This was an open invitation to the Germans to launch a counter-attack in the hope of retaking the village. The invitation was not declined. At least two German counter-attacks were made, the first an hour before midnight and the second four hours later. However, aware of this predictable enemy reaction, 48 Brigade, though low in numbers and battle-weary, prepared for it. The Lewis guns, being issued in increasing numbers to infantry battalions, were deployed in a series of well-sited strongpoints around the brigade front and effective fire from these weapons (capable of between 500 and 600 rounds per minute) broke both counter-attacks while 8th Royal Irish Fusiliers were also moved up to support 48 Brigade. With the Faughs came one of the most famous chaplains of the war, Father Willie Doyle SJ, who described Ginchy as his first real close-quarter sight of a battle, something that he would never forget as every moment he expected 'to be blown into eternity'. Such was Doyle's courage that he was awarded the Military Cross that day.

As well as the counter-attacks the Germans rained artillery fire down on the two brigades of 16th Division during what the new commanding

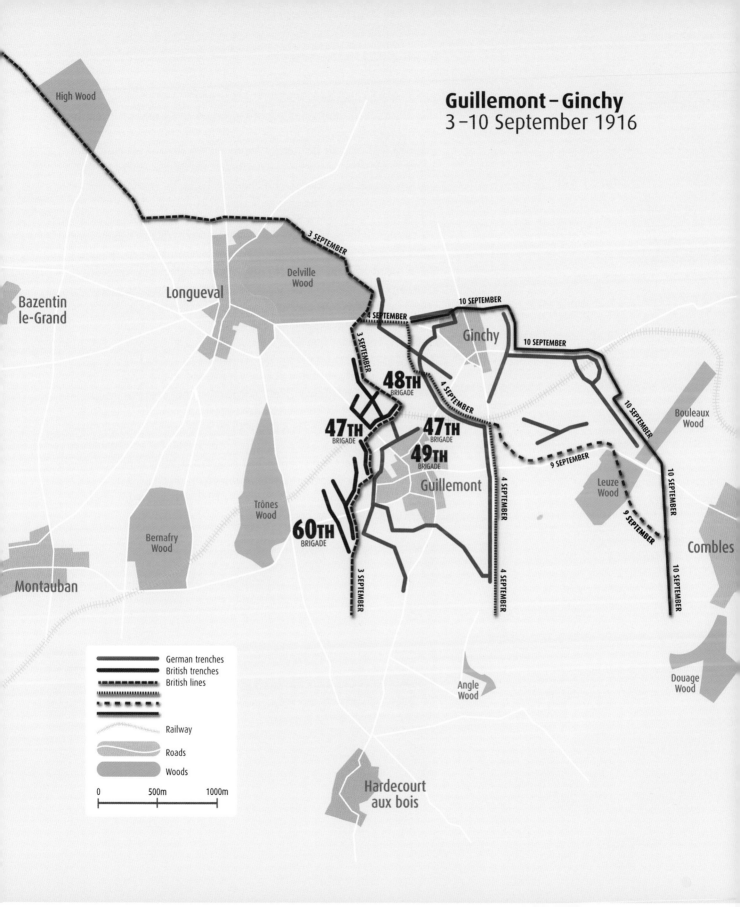

Guillemont–Ginchy
3–10 September 1916

High Wood

Bazentin le-Grand

Longueval

Delville Wood

3 SEPTEMBER

4 SEPTEMBER

3 SEPTEMBER

10 SEPTEMBER

Ginchy

10 SEPTEMBER

10 SEPTEMBER

Bouleaux Wood

48TH BRIGADE

4 SEPTEMBER

47TH BRIGADE

47TH BRIGADE

49TH BRIGADE

Guillemont

9 SEPTEMBER

4 SEPTEMBER

Leuze Wood

9 SEPTEMBER

10 SEPTEMBER

60TH BRIGADE

Trônes Wood

Bernafry Wood

3 SEPTEMBER

4 SEPTEMBER

10 SEPTEMBER

Combles

Montauban

Douage Wood

Angle Wood

Hardecourt aux bois

German trenches
British trenches
British lines

Railway
Roads
Woods

0   500m   1000m

officer of 6th Connaught Rangers, Lieutenant Colonel Rowland Feilding, described as a 'lurid night of countless rockets and star-shells from the enemy, who was nervous at night: a night of wild bursts of machine-gun and rifle fire'. Second Lieutenant Young, of 7th Royal Irish Fusiliers, whose description of the attack is included above, also described that night as Faughs, Inniskillings and Dublins dug in 'by linking up the shell craters'. Even though the men were tired 'they worked with a will, and before long we had got a pretty decent trench outlined'. However, it was a miserable night as everyone was tired, very cold, thirsty and hungry, although some relief from thirst and hunger was obtained by taking black bread, sausage and cold coffee from the packs of the dead Germans. No one was sorry to see the morning when 3 Guards Brigade relieved 16th (Irish) Division with 1st Welsh Guards (formed only in 1915) relieving 48 Brigade at Ginchy.

The *Official History* notes that 'the honour of capturing Ginchy' fell to 48 Brigade plus two battalions of 49, who 'took 200 prisoners but [whose] own losses were very heavy'. Since 1 September 16th Division had suffered 4,330 casualties: of its 435 officers, 240 were dead, wounded or missing; of 10,410 men in its infantry battalions, 4,090 were casualties. In 48 Brigade about half of the force that had gone into action became casualties: twenty-one officers and 170 men had been killed while another sixty-one officers and 1,154 other ranks were wounded or missing. Those losses had included men from all four provinces of Ireland and from the Irish diaspora, the fifth province.

German prisoners taken at Ginchy on the Meaulte-Fricourt road.

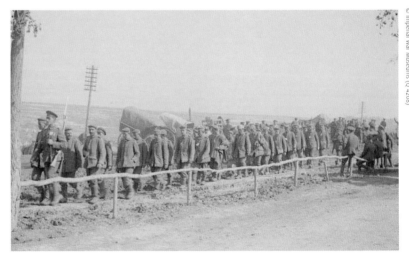

Father Willie Doyle

The Reverend Willie Doyle SJ MC was an Irish Jesuit priest, born in Dalkey in 1873, who volunteered to join the Army Chaplains Department and was appointed as a Catholic chaplain to 16th (Irish) Division, being attached to 8th Royal Irish Fusiliers in 49 Brigade. He was Mentioned in Despatches for his gallant actions during the Battle of Loos when his brigade was caught in a gas attack. Although recommended for a Military Cross this was turned down on the grounds that he had not been at the front long enough.

Father Doyle was awarded the Military Cross for his bravery at Ginchy in September 1916. As was his practice, he went out into no man's land to tend to the wounded and give the last rites to the dying. He earned the admiration of men of all denominations and General Hickie described him as 'one of the bravest men who fought or served out here'.

During the Battle of Messines in June 1917, when 16th (Irish) and 36th (Ulster) Divisions fought in the same corps, Doyle also earned the admiration of the soldiers of the Ulster Division who respected his courage and devotion to duty. By this time, he was attached to 8th Royal Dublin Fusiliers in 48 Brigade, alongside his fellow Jesuit Father Frank Browne, who is remembered as a gifted photographer who sailed on the *Titanic* as far as Queenstown (Cobh). Willie Doyle was recommended for the Distinguished Service Order. No award was made as he was killed less than two months later; the DSO may be conferred only on the living since it is an order.

In the subsequent Battle of Langemarck, part of the Third Battle of Ypres, in August 1917, Willie Doyle was killed while tending wounded in no man's land. He was 44. His grave has been lost but he is remembered on the Tyne Cot Memorial.

Father Doyle was recommended for a posthumous Victoria Cross but this was never awarded. He is also remembered in a stained-glass window in St Finnian's Church, Dromin, County Louth.

Among the dead was an officer who epitomised the best of his generation. Lieutenant Thomas Michael 'Tom' Kettle of 9th Royal Dublin Fusiliers died leading his company into action at Ginchy. The 36-year-old officer had been sent home due to ill health but refused a safe staff posting and persisted in asking to return to France. A former Member of Parliament – he had represented East Tyrone for John Redmond's Irish Party – and professor of national economics at University College, Dublin, Kettle was a true polymath, for he was also a barrister, poet, journalist and writer. A friend of Joyce, Chesterton and Gogarty, he had also been an athlete, cricketer and cyclist at Clongowes Wood College in County Kildare. Kettle had supported the Boers against the British but, caught in Belgium in August 1914 while running arms for the National Volunteers, he saw this war as one of 'civilisation against barbarians' and identified the British, French and Belgians with civilisation and Germany with barbarism. Although angry at the executions of the leaders of the 1916 rebellion in Dublin, he preferred to fight for Ireland in Europe and to die there with his Dubliners. His fellow poet and nationalist George William Russell, known as AE, compared his sacrifice with those who had died in Dublin.

The Hamilton Band

Courtesy St Columb's Cathedral, Londonderry

In 1914 the Hamilton Flute Band, a well-known marching band in Londonderry, which had been formed in 1856, volunteered *en bloc* to join the Derrys. They were joined by bandsmen from a number of other marching bands from the city and the county, including the Maiden City from Rosemount, the No Surrender Band, also from the city, the Parke Band from Coleraine, Portstewart's Burnside Band and Limavady Flute Band. After training at Finner Camp in County Donegal was complete, the Hamiltons became the regimental band for the battalion and accompanied them to France. When in action the bandsmen generally acted as stretcher-bearers and in the regimental aid post; in each battalion 16 bandsmen usually acted as stretcher-

bearers. The band's drums were used for field services. These were military drums, rather than the band's own instruments but, after the war, the Royal Inniskilling Fusiliers presented them to the band. The bass drum, as well as a number of side drums, were laid up in St Columb's Cathedral and today may be seen in the Chapterhouse.

A number of bandsmen lost their lives and the Hamilton Flute Band continues to mark their memory on 1 July each year with a wreathlaying service at Londonderry's War Memorial.

Courtesy Gardiner S. Mitchell

You who have fought on fields afar
That other Ireland did you wrong
Who said you shadowed Ireland's star,
Nor gave you laurel wreath nor song.
You proved by death as true as they,
In mightier conflicts played your part,
Equal your sacrifice may weigh,
Dear Kettle of the generous heart.[14]

Days before his death in action, Kettle had written a sonnet, dedicated to his daughter, Betty, which serves as an epitaph not only for him, but for all who died:

In wiser days, my darling rosebud, blown
To beauty proud as was your mother's prime,
In that desired, delayed, incredible time,
You'll ask why I abandoned you, my own,
And the dear heart that was your baby throne,
To dice with death. And oh! they'll give you rhyme
And reason: some will call the thing sublime,
And some decry it in a knowing tone.
So here, while the mad guns curse overhead,
And tired men sigh with mud for couch and floor,
Know that we fools, now with the foolish dead,
Died not for flag, nor King, nor Emperor –
But for a dream, born in a herdsman's shed,
And for the secret Scripture of the poor.

Tom Kettle has no known grave and is commemorated on the Thiepval Memorial.

Ramsay, of 48 Brigade, wrote that, for soldiers who had been out in trenches that were really only shell holes for five days and nights before the attack on Ginchy, soaked by rain and without hot food:

the highest credit is reflected on all ranks, that the capture of Ginchy was effected under these adverse conditions, and that the traditions of the Irish race were worthily upheld by these men of the New Armies.

Elsewhere on 9 September Wood Lane was captured on 1st Division's front while in High Wood bitter fighting occurred that involved both

---

[14] From 'To The Memory of Some I knew Who are Dead and Who loved Ireland'.

1st Northamptons and 2nd Munsters. The latter's history notes the conditions endured by the battalion:

> High Wood … had already changed hands several times, and the whole battlefield was churned up into a network of shell-holes and trenches. The British artillery was greatly hampered by the absence of roads, most of them having been blown out of existence.

The artillery was also suffering from severe wear to the barrels of the guns. It being impossible to bring up new guns, bombardments became more and more inaccurate, so much so that the front area was sometimes evacuated to a depth of almost a mile. The Munsters were withdrawn on 12 September but it was now the turn of another Irish battalion to enter the fray.

On the night of 13/14 September 2nd Irish Guards, of 2 Guards Brigade, went into action near Ginchy. The Guards had been transferred from the Ypres salient in August and, on 9 September, relieved 4th Grenadiers who, it may be remembered, had earlier relieved 47 Brigade. Their first duty in the line was to hunt down some enemy machine-gun posts. No.2 Company was detailed for the task. Even as they moved across the Ginchy-Morval road to the position from which they would make their attack, casualties were suffered from enfilading machine-gun fire. Then it was found that the wire had not been cut effectively:

> And when the attack was launched, in waves of two platoons each, undisturbed machine guns in a few dreadful moments accounted for more than three-quarters of the little host. Almost at the outset, Lieutenant Montgomery was killed close to our own parapet, and those who were left, under 2nd Lieutenant Hely-Hutchinson, lay down till they might crawl back after dark. That wiped out No.2 Company, and, next day, its thirty survivors were sent back to the first-line Transport – a bleak prelude to the battle itself.

The Irish Guards settled down to await the coming battle.

What did 16th (Irish) Division's success at Guillemont and Ginchy mean in strategic terms? The attacks on the two villages were not intended simply to seize them for the sake of taking more ground but to ensure that the next phase of operations on the Somme front could be launched from a better jumping-off ground. That phase, the third and final of the Somme campaign, would begin with the battle for Flers-Courcelette and feature the first use of a new weapon, the tank.

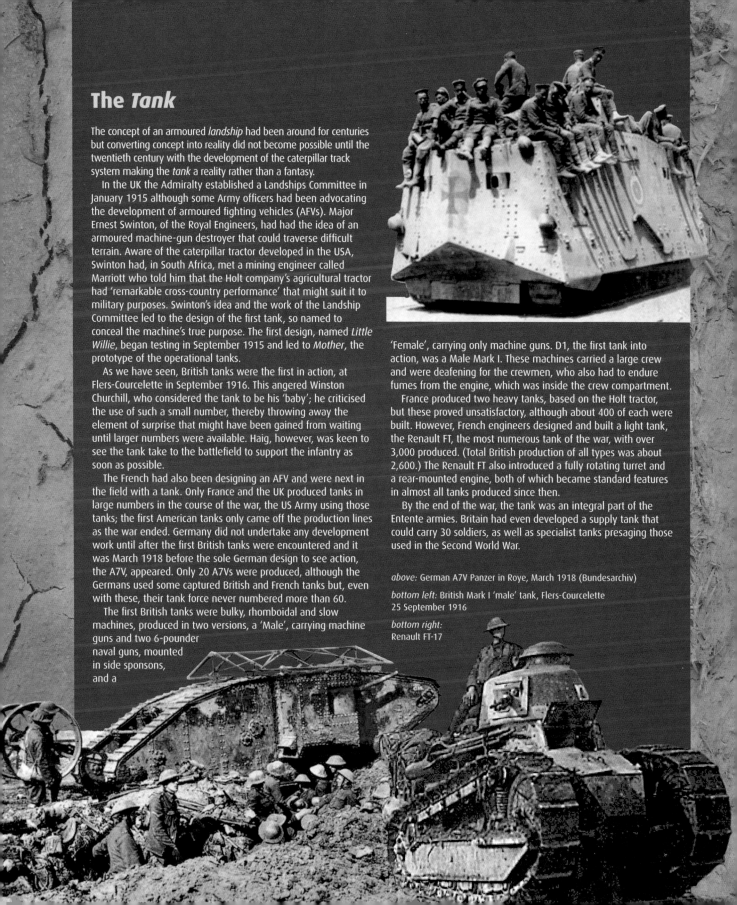

The *Tank*

The concept of an armoured *landship* had been around for centuries but converting concept into reality did not become possible until the twentieth century with the development of the caterpillar track system making the *tank* a reality rather than a fantasy.

In the UK the Admiralty established a Landships Committee in January 1915 although some Army officers had been advocating the development of armoured fighting vehicles (AFVs). Major Ernest Swinton, of the Royal Engineers, had had the idea of an armoured machine-gun destroyer that could traverse difficult terrain. Aware of the caterpillar tractor developed in the USA, Swinton had, in South Africa, met a mining engineer called Marriott who told him that the Holt company's agricultural tractor had 'remarkable cross-country performance' that might suit it to military purposes. Swinton's idea and the work of the Landship Committee led to the design of the first tank, so named to conceal the machine's true purpose. The first design, named *Little Willie*, began testing in September 1915 and led to *Mother*, the prototype of the operational tanks.

As we have seen, British tanks were the first in action, at Flers-Courcelette in September 1916. This angered Winston Churchill, who considered the tank to be his 'baby'; he criticised the use of such a small number, thereby throwing away the element of surprise that might have been gained from waiting until larger numbers were available. Haig, however, was keen to see the tank take to the battlefield to support the infantry as soon as possible.

The French had also been designing an AFV and were next in the field with a tank. Only France and the UK produced tanks in large numbers in the course of the war, the US Army using those tanks; the first American tanks only came off the production lines as the war ended. Germany did not undertake any development work until after the first British tanks were encountered and it was March 1918 before the sole German design to see action, the A7V, appeared. Only 20 A7Vs were produced, although the Germans used some captured British and French tanks but, even with these, their tank force never numbered more than 60.

The first British tanks were bulky, rhomboidal and slow machines, produced in two versions, a 'Male', carrying machine guns and two 6-pounder naval guns, mounted in side sponsons, and a 'Female', carrying only machine guns. D1, the first tank into action, was a Male Mark I. These machines carried a large crew and were deafening for the crewmen, who also had to endure fumes from the engine, which was inside the crew compartment.

France produced two heavy tanks, based on the Holt tractor, but these proved unsatisfactory, although about 400 of each were built. However, French engineers designed and built a light tank, the Renault FT, the most numerous tank of the war, with over 3,000 produced. (Total British production of all types was about 2,600.) The Renault FT also introduced a fully rotating turret and a rear-mounted engine, both of which became standard features in almost all tanks produced since then.

By the end of the war, the tank was an integral part of the Entente armies. Britain had even developed a supply tank that could carry 30 soldiers, as well as specialist tanks presaging those used in the Second World War.

above: German A7V Panzer in Roye, March 1918 (Bundesarchiv)

bottom left: British Mark I 'male' tank, Flers-Courcelette 25 September 1916

bottom right: Renault FT-17

7 The Final Months

General Haig hoped that a renewed offensive, using the new 'secret weapon', the tank, could achieve a breakthrough of the German defences, leading to a breakout in which the cavalry could be employed in fluid open warfare. Haig was an enthusiastic proponent of the tank, as he was of air power, and had wanted to use tanks for the opening of the campaign in July. His hopes for a mass tank attack were dashed by the fact that the manufacturers of the 'land battleship' could not produce enough of them in time.

Although the concept of an armoured fighting vehicle, able to overcome obstacles such as ditches, trenches and broken terrain, was not new, work on a viable vehicle had begun only in February 1915 with the creation of the Landships Committee, a body taken over from the Admiralty by the War Office in summer 1915. A prototype 'tank', as it was codenamed to ensure secrecy, began trials in January 1916. Intended to break the stasis of trench warfare, it found an early supporter in Haig, who had recently become commander of the BEF.

By September some tanks were available for the BEF and Haig had Rawlinson incorporate them in the plans for Fourth Army's attack at Flers-Courcelette. However, this would be no easy introduction to active service for the new weapon as the ground over which they would have to operate was broken by trenches, shell holes and bomb craters as well as the natural contours. Moreover, the men who were to crew the noisy, awkward vehicles had no experience in operating their tanks in anything approaching operational conditions, while the tanks themselves still suffered many mechanical problems. In spite of all these caveats, including the fact that only forty-nine were available, Haig was still keen to use them. It was believed that the tanks could support the infantry, particularly by destroying wire and dealing with machine-gun posts.

Others were opposed to their use, including the French, mainly because they believed that the tank should be kept secret until there were sufficient to deploy in a mass attack that would have a much better chance of creating a breakthrough. Haig's view prevailed and the tanks were deployed for the offensive at Flers-Courcelette. Kipling, in his history of 2nd Irish Guards notes that, on 9 September, the battalion, while waiting at Happy Valley to begin the relief of 4th Grenadiers, 'had their first sight of the tanks, some thirty of which were parked, trumpeting and clanking, near their camp'.

September was not to be the most propitious month for offensive operations on the Somme front. The month was wet and the rain proved a major element in the battles that followed. However, the new German high commanders, von Hindenburg and Ludendorff, had called off the Verdun offensive at the end of August,[15] thus allowing reinforcement of German forces along the Somme; more artillery was moved to the front. Although the Brusilov Offensive was still tying down large numbers of German troops on the Eastern Front, the end of offensive operations at Verdun was to the advantage of those defending against the French and British on the Somme.

Flers-Courcelette was also the battle in which the Canadian Corps made its debut while, for the New Zealand Division, formed in Egypt on 1 March 1916, this was to be the first major offensive action; it had seen defensive action and had taken part in raiding since its arrival on the Western Front. Part of II Australian and New Zealand Army Corps (II ANZAC), the New Zealand Division was detached to XV Corps for this operation. This was to be the third and final effort to break through the German lines in the Somme campaign.

Z Day was 15 September with a total of eleven British and Dominion divisions committed. As well as 2nd Irish Guards, the Micks' 1st Battalion would also be involved, while 2nd Munsters had a peripheral involvement, as did 4th (Royal Irish) Dragoon Guards and 8th (King's Royal Irish) Hussars. The Territorial Force soldiers of the London Irish Rifles were also committed at High Wood. Both Irish Guards battalions were serving in the Guards Division but in different brigades, 1st with 1 Guards Brigade and 2nd with 2 Guards Brigade. The Guards Division attacked towards

---

[15] The fighting at Verdun did not end then but continued until December.

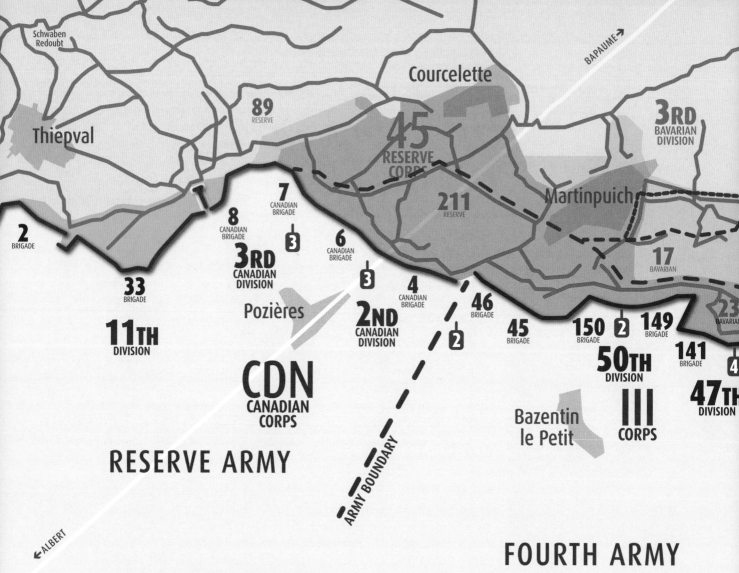

Schwaben
Redoubt

Thiepval

Courcelette

BAPAUME →

89
RESERVE

45
RESERVE
CORPS

3RD
BAVARIAN
DIVISION

2
BRIGADE

8
CANADIAN
BRIGADE

7
CANADIAN
BRIGADE

3

3RD
CANADIAN
DIVISION

6
CANADIAN
BRIGADE

3

4
CANADIAN
BRIGADE

211
RESERVE

Martinpuich

17
BAVARIAN

33
BRIGADE

Pozières

2ND
CANADIAN
DIVISION

46
BRIGADE

2

45
BRIGADE

150
BRIGADE

2

149
BRIGADE

23
BAVARIAN

11TH
DIVISION

CDN
CANADIAN
CORPS

2

Bazentin
le Petit

141
BRIGADE

4

50TH
DIVISION

III
CORPS

47TH
DIVISION

RESERVE ARMY

ARMY BOUNDARY

← ALBERT

FOURTH ARMY

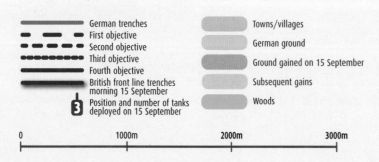

Battle of Flers-Courcelette
15–22 September 1916

——— German trenches	Towns/villages
– – – First objective	German ground
–·–·– Second objective	Ground gained on 15 September
Third objective	Subsequent gains
Fourth objective	Woods
British front line trenches morning 15 September	
3 Position and number of tanks deployed on 15 September	

0   1000m   2000m   3000m

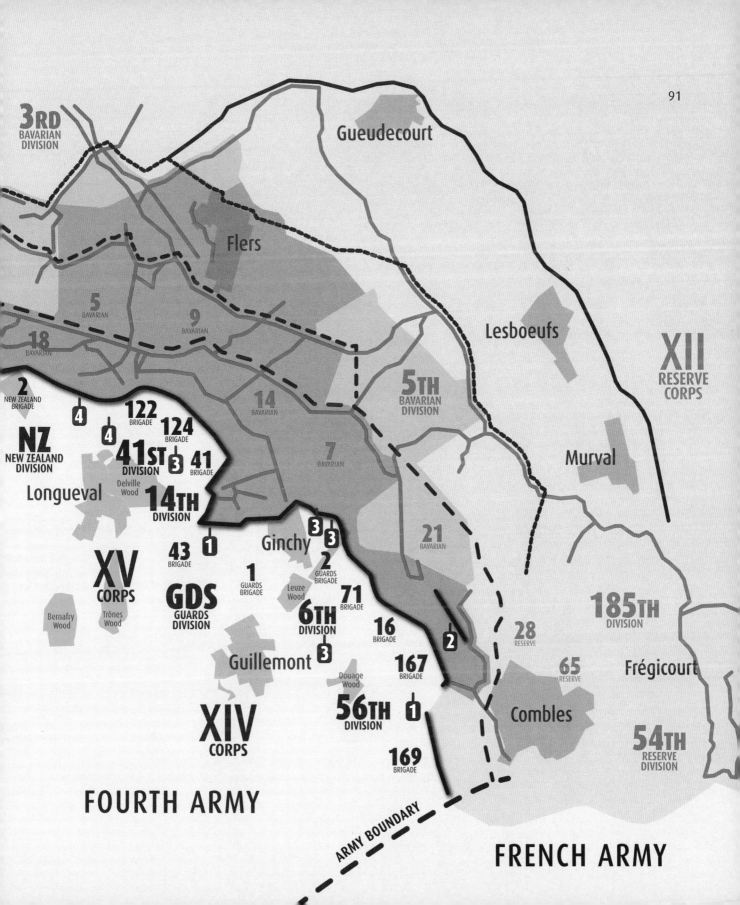

3RD BAVARIAN DIVISION

Gueudecourt

Flers

5 BAVARIAN

9 BAVARIAN

18 BAVARIAN

Lesboeufs

XII RESERVE CORPS

2 NEW ZEALAND BRIGADE

4

122 BRIGADE

4

124 BRIGADE

NZ NEW ZEALAND DIVISION

41ST DIVISION

3

41 BRIGADE

14 BAVARIAN

5TH BAVARIAN DIVISION

7 BAVARIAN

Murval

Longueval

Delville Wood

14TH DIVISION

Ginchy

3

3

21 BAVARIAN

XV CORPS

43 BRIGADE

1

1 GUARDS BRIGADE

Leuze Wood

2 GUARDS BRIGADE

185TH DIVISION

Bernafry Wood

Trônes Wood

GDS GUARDS DIVISION

6TH DIVISION

71 BRIGADE

16 BRIGADE

28 RESERVE

65 RESERVE

Frégicourt

3

Guillemont

Douage Wood

2

167 BRIGADE

Combles

XIV CORPS

56TH DIVISION

1

54TH RESERVE DIVISION

169 BRIGADE

FOURTH ARMY

ARMY BOUNDARY

FRENCH ARMY

Lesboeufs (or les Boeufs) from Ginchy with 2 Brigade on the right and 1 Brigade on the left.

The Guards' attack on the right saw 2 Brigade penetrating into parts of the Triangle and Serpentine Trench and taking 200 prisoners. With No.2 Company all but wiped out, 2nd Irish Guards distributed the men of No.3 Company between Nos.1 and 4 Companies to attack in two enlarged waves. As so often before, there was a night-long wait for Zero Hour, during which the German artillery bombarded what they believed to be the British assembly areas, between Guillemont and Ginchy. However, 2 Guards Brigade were elsewhere, thanks to reconnoitring work carried out by Major Rocke and Captain the Honourable Harold Alexander, who had advised a different assembly area. Alexander, from Caledon in County Tyrone, was to receive every gallantry decoration bar the Victoria Cross, rise to be an acting brigade commander by the end of the war and to be a field marshal in the next war. Known popularly as 'Alex' he was to be one of the most famous soldiers of the twentieth century.

The 2 Brigade attack was led by 3rd Grenadiers and 1st Coldstream, who were checked by 'a string of shell-holes' manned by Germans who had survived the British artillery bombardment. This delayed the advance for a time and meant that the Irish Guards came up on the heels of the first wave, the overall effect being to swing the brigade axis leftward and into 1 Brigade. The latter had had their own problems. Exacerbating the tactical situation was the fact that 6th Division, to the right of 2 Guards Brigade, had been held up by heavy machine-gun fire from the German defensive position known as the Quadrilateral, which dominated that end of the line. This had the effect of further 'bending' leftward the axis of 2 Guards Brigade.

It became more difficult to know where a unit was. Kipling describes the ground:

> The drawback was that the whole landscape happened to be one pitted, clodded, brown and white wilderness of aching uniformity, on which to pick up any given detail was like identifying one plover's nest in a hundred-acre bog.

However, the Guards are noted for their ability to adapt to the local situation and in 'due time, and no man can say what actually happened outside his own range of action, for no man saw anything coherently, their general advance reached the German trench which was their first objective'. With fire from the Quadrilateral and from Germans in the rear, whose trenches had been overrun but not eliminated, the first objective proved 'none too bad a refuge even if we had to bomb ourselves into it'. Captain Alexander had distinguished himself, along with Second Lieutenant Greer, as both had taken care of the Germans in the first unexpected trench. Of the nine tanks that were to support the Guards Division there was no sign, nor of the cavalry who were to take Bapaume.

Heavy fighting continued and a mixed party of about a hundred Grenadier, Scots and Irish Guards almost reached Lesboeufs. After repelling a German counter-attack, this group was forced to withdraw. Prominent within it, not surprisingly, were Major Rocke, Captain Alexander and Lieutenant Greer. Meanwhile, the 1st Battalion, commanded by Lieutenant Colonel McCalmont, captured part of the second objective, some of which was outside the corps boundary. A group of Irish Guards, under CSM Carton and Sergeant Riordan DCM, had pushed beyond the objective and were in touch with men of 9th Rifle Brigade to their left, a unit of XIV Corps. Their right was in the air and there was uncertainty about where the trench in which they lay actually was. Its position was fixed by taking compass bearings:

It was more or less on the line of the second objective, and had therefore to be held in spite of casualties. The men could do no more than fire when possible at anything that showed itself (which was seldom) and, in the rare intervals when shelling slackened, work themselves a little farther into the ground.

As the day wore on, Captain Hargreaves, who had been left behind with the reserve in Trônes Wood, arrived and, although wounded, led out a mixed group of Coldstream and Irish to a line of shell holes some few hundred yards forward of the trench. These disconnected shelters provided protection from shell and machine-gun fire throughout the afternoon. A machine-gun detachment and some more Coldstream and Irish arrived as reinforcements but further advance was impossible. Any movement attracted fire and, with nearly every officer dead or wounded, sergeant after sergeant took command but they too succumbed to enemy fire and command devolved on the corporals. Although the battalion had been cut to pieces its discipline held 'and with it the instinct that made them crawl, dodge, run and stumble as chance offered and their Corporals ordered, towards the enemy and not away from him'.

With no communication with Brigade HQ, 1st Irish Guards lacked all the necessities for battle. The last machine gun was knocked out and, as the sun set, a counter-attack appeared to be massing. It did not occur but an attack by 2nd Scots Guards was witnessed. That failed but some of the Scots joined the Coldstream and the Irish in their trench while some of the men in the forward trench were able to make their way back. Under cover of darkness it was possible to send out scouts and contact was made with battalions to either flank while water and rations appeared, as if by some miracle. Other survivors and stragglers also found the position which was indicated by flares to friendly aircraft.

Throughout the next day and night the Micks endured their isolation until a company of Lincolns from 62 Brigade arrived to relieve them. There had been over 340 casualties in 1st Irish Guards and 1,776 in 1 Guards Brigade. Among the Micks' dead was the gallant Lieutenant James Macgregor Greer MC of Ballymoney, County Antrim, who died of his wounds on 3 October.

> No one seems to recall accurately the order of events between the gathering in Bernafay Wood and the arrival of the shadow of the Battalion in camp at the Citadel. The sun was shining; breakfast was ready for the officers and men near some trees. It struck their very tired apprehensions that there was an enormous amount of equipage and service for a very few men, and they noticed dully a sudden hustling off of unneeded plates and cups. They felt as though they had returned to a world which had outgrown them on a somewhat terrifying scale during all the ages that they had been away from it. Their one need, after food had been eaten sitting, was rest, and, when the first stupor of exhaustion was satisfied, their sleep began to be broken by dreams only less horrible than the memories to which they waked.

In his letter of thanks to the Micks the brigade commander, Brigadier General Pereira, wrote that:

> The advance from the Orchard in the face of machine-gun fire is equal to anything you have yet accomplished in this campaign, and once more the 1st Battalion Irish Guards has carried out a most magnificent advance and held ground gained in spite of the most severe losses.

In 47th (1/2nd London) Division the London Irish Rifles took part in the attack that seized from the Germans the final part of High Wood that had been under their control; losses were high in 47th Division. Although the attack was supported by four tanks, the battle for High Wood was bloody, every piece of ground having to be fought for against soldiers who were well sited for defence with machine guns in concrete strongpoints causing many casualties. Clearing High Wood was 'a great achievement on the part of the London Irish' who would continue to fight in actions subsequent to Flers-Courcelette, including the capture of Eaucourt l'Abbaye.

Haig had hoped that the breakthrough would be made in the southern part of the line, on his right flank, with Rawlinson's Fourth Army. However, the German defences at the Quadrilateral proved too strong and inflicted heavy losses on the attackers from 6th and 56th (London) Divisions. Not until the 18th did 6th Division take the Quadrilateral, allowing the Guards Division to make further progress. The attacks in this sector had faltered for a number of reasons: poor weather prevented aircraft from flying and restricted observation for the artillery observers which, in turn, meant that the attackers were uncertain of the exact positions of the German trenches in the Quadrilateral. With the Quadrilateral subdued, Guards Division were able to advance some 2,000 yards but were stopped short of their final objective, Lesboeufs.

On the left flank, in the northern sector, the Canadians, in Gough's Reserve Army (later renamed Fifth Army), made considerable progress, advancing over a mile on the first day to take their objectives in and around the village of Courcelette. For the next four days the Germans made many attempts to recapture the village, which was subjected to heavy bombardment, but the Canadian troops, although cut off and with diminishing supplies of food and water, held out. Although none of the Canadian units was identifiably Irish, one of the NCOs of the 29th (Vancouver) Battalion would go on to earn the Victoria Cross a year later. Robert Hill Hanna, from Aughnahoory, near Kilkeel in County Down, had emigrated to Canada in 1905 and joined the Canadian forces on the outbreak of war. He would earn the VC at Lens in September 1917, by which time he was also a warrant officer.

In Fourth Army the New Zealand Division had also met with early success, capturing the switch line between High Wood and Flers after thirty minutes of fighting. This division also numbered many Irish soldiers amongst its ranks with one estimate from New Zealand officials putting the number of Irish-born New Zealand servicemen of the First World War at over 50 per cent of those who served.

Reverend James Gilbert Paton

The Reverend James Gilbert Paton MC** MiD served as a chaplain to 109 Brigade's 10th Royal Inniskilling Fusiliers, the Derrys. A Presbyterian minister who had served in Coleraine and volunteered to join the Army Chaplains Department in 1914, he sought and obtained a posting to the Derrys, his local unit, from 16th Royal Irish Rifles. An old boy of Foyle College, Londonderry, which has an annual languages prize in his name, he ended the war with the Military Cross and two Bars, as well as a Mention in Despatches.

Paton's first MC was earned in July 1916 on the Somme. His commanding officer, Macrory, described how a party of Derrys was sent out to search for surviving wounded in no man's land on the night of 2 July. 'Our own party was in charge of our padre, Capt. J. J. (sic) Paton MC and did splendid work. Paton got the MC for this (and later on a Bar for further gallantry). No citation was published for this award which was not gazetted until 1 June 1917, almost a year later.

His first Bar was awarded for helping to evacuate wounded under heavy shell and machine-gun fire during which, on one occasion, he helped carry a seriously-wounded man four miles to an aid station, showing 'fine disregard for personal safety and devotion to duty'. This award was gazetted only three days after his first award. His second Bar was awarded for operations during October 1918 when he again did not spare himself in tending to the wounded, ignoring shells and machine-gun fire to do so. 'His gallant conduct and untiring efforts were admirable.' This award was gazetted on 29 July 1919. No record of his Mention in Despatches survives.

The Reverend Paton had originally gone to France with the YMCA. A married man, he appears in the 1911 census of Ireland as a 28-year-old minister in Newry with two children under the age of two. The Newry ministry explains his being posted to 16th Rifles, a Down battalion.

He survived the war and returned to the ministry becoming Moderator of the Presbyterian Church in 1931. In 1935–36 he was President of Foyle College Old Boys' Association.

Courtesy the London Gazette

LONDON GAZETTE, 30 DECEMBER, 1915.

ARMY CHAPLAINS DEPARTMENT

The undermentioned to be temporary Chaplains to the Forces, 4th Class:—

Dated 11th December, 1915.
The Reverend James Gilbert Paton.

LONDON GAZETTE, 16 SEPTEMBER, 1918.

Rev. James Gilbert Paton, M.C., A. Chapln. Dept.

For conspicuous gallantry and devotion to duty. Under heavy shell and machine-gun fire he helped to evacuate wounded, and in one instance helped to carry a serious wounded case four miles to an aid station. He showed fine disregard for personal safety and devotion to duty.
(M.C. gazetted 4th June, 1917.)

LONDON GAZETTE, 15 FEBRUARY, 1919.

AWARDED A SECOND BAR TO THE MILITARY CROSS.

Rev. James Gilbert Paton, M.C., Army Chap. Dept., attd. 2nd Bn., R. Innis. Fus.
(M.C. gazetted 4th June, 1917.)
(1st Bar gazetted 16th September, 1918.)

Mention in Despatches symbol:
a bronze oak leaf spray.

The battle of Flers-Courcelette ended on 22 September and plans for a Franco-British attack on the 21st were postponed until the 25th; Sixth French Army had been in action, with its artillery supporting British attacks, and Tenth Army had also attacked with some success on 15 and 17 September but lack of reserves had prevented exploitation of that success.

The tanks had not proved to be a battle-winning weapon, although their psychological effect on German infantry was significant, intimidating those who faced them and acting as a morale booster for British infantry. Mechanical problems had played a part, although the small number available meant that they could not be decisive. Only thirty-two of the forty-nine tanks reached their start lines where a further seven failed to start, so that only twenty-five moved into battle. Most of those bogged down in the difficult terrain, or suffered mechanical breakdown, so that only nine penetrated the enemy lines. Walking infantry proved faster than the tanks. Winston Churchill, who had headed the Landships Committee, was critical of the use of tanks in small numbers 'for the mere purpose of taking a few ruined villages'. However, the problems that had shown themselves in battlefield conditions prompted improvements in tank design and the development of better tactics, which helped make the tank an important weapon in the closing years of the war.

On 25 September Fourth Army's offensive was renewed in the battle of Morval. The objectives were Morval, Gueudecourt and Lesboeufs, held by the German First Army, which had been the final objectives in the battle of Flers-Courcelette. The main attack was planned to coincide with attacks by Sixth French Army on Combles, south of Morval, to close up to the enemy positions between Moislains and le Transloy. This combined attack, from the Somme river northwards to Martinpuich, had a further purpose: to prevent the Germans reinforcing their defence at Thiepval before the Reserve Army launched an attack on Thiepval ridge on 26 September.

On the Fourth Army front, the Guards Division advanced on the left of XIV Corps. Once again, both battalions of the Irish Guards deployed, the 1st Battalion having been reinforced to almost 600 all ranks by the 20th. That created the problem of launching a battalion, 'more than half untried recruits, across the open against all that organised death can deliver'.

As they waited to be committed to battle the guardsmen suffered shelling and spent some of their time clearing the detritus of battle. Plans for 25 September were less ambitious than for ten days earlier: the distance to the first objective was some 300 yards, to the second 800 and to the third 1,300. 'In each case the objective [was] a clearly defined one, and not merely a line drawn across the map.' The Micks' tasks were to clear the three objectives, supported by 3rd Coldstream, 'to clean out the northern portion of Lesboeufs village, and above all to secure their flanks when they halted or were held up'.

Infantry await the order to attack at Morval. The difference in the front-line trenches is clear from this photograph: the well-constructed trenches predating Z Day have given way to temporary, and often hasty, excavations.

Nos.1 and 2 Companies formed the first wave of 1st Irish Guards to advance at Zero Hour and, with excellent support from the artillery, were soon on the first enemy line where they found only dazed men anxious to be made prisoner and taken out of the hell they were suffering. Nos.3 and 4 Companies had followed up, although they had sustained casualties

from a German bombardment of their front and communication trenches
as they waited to follow the first wave. Although 2nd Grenadiers on the
left had suffered heavily while working their way through wire concealed
by high corn, they maintained contact and the integrity of the advance
was ensured. Both battalions then made for Lesboeufs, some 500 yards
ahead. The village was taken and the attackers set off for the final
objective, just east of Lesboeufs and east of a sunken road.

The final surge forward included a rush across uprooted orchards and
through wrecked houses, shops and barns, with buildings alight or
confusedly collapsing round them, and the enemy streaming out ahead
to hide in shell-holes in the open.

Thanks to the artillery and, to a lesser extent, the tanks, there had been
much less machine-gun fire than might have been the case and casualties
were lower. The Micks and Grenadiers now dug in while the guns
hammered the open land beyond Lesboeufs. Sadly, the new positions
came under fire from British artillery and a number of casualties resulted
with Captain Hargreaves, who had distinguished himself ten days earlier,
wounded fatally and Captain Drury-Lowe of the Grenadiers killed, both
by the same shell. The battalion suffered 250 casualties and was relieved
by 2nd Irish Guards on the 26th. In its turn the 2nd Battalion suffered
regular bombardment until relieved on the night of the 28th by 1st
Coldstream. On 2 October the Guards Division was withdrawn from
the line for intensive training. The Irish Guards' part in the Somme
campaign was over.

On 26 September the Reserve Army opened the battle for Thiepval Ridge,
which had been under artillery bombardment for three days. The village
and its plateau had defied attack since 1 July. In this operation, involving
Canadian and British troops, the Germans defended desperately but
to no avail. The ridge fell to the attackers and the defenders had suffered
horrendous casualties by the end of the battle on 28 September. Although
no Irish units were involved in this battle, another Irish Victoria Cross
was gained. Private Frederick Jeremiah Edwards was serving in 12th
Middlesex Regiment, known as the 'Diehards', in 54 Brigade of 18th
(Eastern) Division. The battalion was assigned the task of taking
Thiepval village on the 26th and, with the support of two tanks, made
good progress. However, later in the day, during a critical phase in the
operation, B Company was held up by heavy fire from a machine-gun

99

position. All the company officers became casualties and there was every possibility that the attack was about to be beaten off. At that point Private Edwards charged towards the machine gun, attacked it with hand grenades and knocked it out, allowing the advance to continue. By the end of the day 54 Brigade had made a successful advance across a mile of stoutly-defended ground. Edwards was recommended for the VC, which was gazetted on 25 November. Born in Queenstown, now Cobh, the son of a Royal Garrison Artillery gunner, he had enlisted in the RGA in 1908 but later transferred to the Middlesex Regiment.

During this period the South Irish Horse, XV Corps' cavalry regiment, took part in a brief mounted action. On 26 September the Horse and 19th Lancers (Fane's Horse) of the Indian Army advanced from Mametz. Crossing trenches manned by British troops, they traversed the open country near Flers at a trot before coming under shellfire and pushing mounted patrols into Gueudecourt, where they dismounted and opened fire on the enemy with their Hotchkiss machine guns and rifles. The cavalry held their positions in the face of an advance by three enemy infantry battalions. Not until British infantry arrived in Gueudecourt that evening to relieve them did they leave those positions.

Fourth Army hoped to achieve significant success during October before the onset of winter closed down major operations but the weather proved fickle and blunted the effect of October's operations. Nonetheless, the month saw two major battles begin on the 1st, both of which would last until 11 November. These were the battles for le Transloy and the Ancre Heights. In the first, three Irish battalions, 1st Royal Irish Fusiliers, 2nd Royal Dublin Fusiliers, both in 10 Brigade of 4th Division, and 1st London Irish Rifles, in 141 Brigade of 47th Division, took part while one unit, 1st Royal Irish Rifles, fought on the Ancre Heights.

As a prelude to the Transloy offensive 1st London Irish took part in an attack that saw them bomb their way up Flers Trench on 29 September. On the last day of the month the Rifles pushed the Germans back beyond Flers Switch, close to Eaucourt l'Abbaye, where they were engaged heavily on 2 October. Their time on the Somme front ended a week later when 47th Division was relieved.

On the 12th the Faughs attacked alongside French troops at Transloy, having carried out practice attacks in training. As they moved into the line, they found that 10 Brigade was on the extreme right of the British line; the battalion had only the Royal Warwicks between them and their French allies. Their move forward was seen by the Germans who 'put down a moderate barrage' that caused some casualties. As they waited for their attack on the German lines to begin, the Faughs suffered more casualties from shellfire. 'The object of the attack on 12 October was to establish a position from which the enemy's main line at le Transloy could be assaulted, but it was not a success from the Battalion point of view.'

Zero Hour was 2.05pm and, as the bombardment started, the soldiers left their trenches to begin the advance. Unfortunately, they were too eager to get forward and followed the moving bombardment too closely which led to casualties and a momentary halt. That halt, although brief, was sufficient for German machine guns at a strongpoint about 500 yards from Lesboeufs to come into action against the Faughs. The strongpoint had not been knocked out by the bombardment and its defenders had taken advantage of this. Moreover, it sat on the boundary line between the Faughs and the Warwicks, an error in planning that meant that neither unit had clear responsibility for dealing with it. Although the Faughs made valiant efforts to resume their advance, these were in vain as the machine-gun fire continued to pin them down. Eventually, 10 Brigade's commander ordered the attacking battalions to consolidate and hold the old front line. This was done and patrolling was carried out that indicated that the Germans were also in their forward positions. The Faughs had sustained heavy losses with companies reduced to an average of fifty-four all ranks; A Company had only thirty-nine men while the strongest was B with sixty-four.

Although 1st Royal Irish Fusiliers remained in the line and were ordered to act as brigade support for a 4th Division attack on 23 October, that attack was successful and the battalion was not called forward. French troops had captured Sailly-Saillisel just days before and this had been a help to 4th Division's attack as the village flanked the strongpoint that had earlier created such problems. The battalion was withdrawn before the end of the month and moved to billets out of the line. Between 9 and 14 October inclusive, casualties had totalled 385 while, two days later, the battalion could muster only 427 officers and men.

In the Ancre Heights battle 8th Division was deployed in an attack that was intended to 'get within striking distance of the village of le Transloy, on the Bapaume-Peronne road, from the present position between Morval and Lesboeufs'. Although the three main German lines that had existed on 1 July had all been penetrated, the Germans had been able to create strong defences as they fell back, either by digging in, wiring or by a combination of both. Eighth Division's attack was to be made with 23 Brigade on the right, 25 in the centre and 24 on the left; 1st Royal Irish Rifles were still in 25 Brigade.

The first of two objectives for 25 Brigade was represented partly by Zenith Trench which continued 'an imaginary line' to the left to Misty Trench in the British line. Another 300 yards farther on lay the second objective. Poor weather delayed Zero Hour from 9.30am to 2.30pm on 22 October. Both leading battalions, 2nd Lincolns and 2nd Rifle Brigade, were brought to a standstill by withering machine-gun and rifle fire although on the left flank of the Rifle Brigade the objective was attained. The Royal Irish Rifles were the supporting battalion in this attack and, at Zero Hour, moved up to occupy Spider and Rainbow Trenches, vacated by 2nd Royal Berkshires. As usual, the German artillery shelled the area through which they knew supporting troops would be moving but the Rifles suffered little loss from the bombardment. However, as the battalion crossed the Sunken Road it was a different story with the shells taking a heavy toll of the riflemen. Even in the forward trenches there were many casualties from shellfire, the trenches generally being shallow.

Orders were received to assault Zenith Trench, with Zero Hour being 3.50am on 24 October. However, the ground, already difficult, was made even more so as rain fell that evening and during the night. A and B Companies of the Rifles were in line left of the Berkshires and, because of the condition of the ground, both battalions stepped off just before Zero so that they might keep close to the creeping bombardment. This precaution was in vain. The attackers had advanced only seventy yards when they were assailed by vicious machine-gun and rifle fire from Zenith Trench, which was defended strongly by the Germans. That fire brought the attack to a standstill. Both battalions retreated, having suffered heavy losses: from 23 to 26 October, the Rifles lost 218 casualties, of whom twenty-one had been killed.

The divisional attack had achieved some success but the Germans still held 250 yards of trench. Three companies of the Rifles were ordered to hold the front line with the fourth, and two companies of Sherwood

Foresters, in support while the other battalions were withdrawn to re-organise. Those in the front line endured regular shelling until, on the 26th, 1st Royal Irish Rifles were relieved. Two days later they were back in the line in Spider Trench, but only two companies strong, awaiting a fresh attack that was postponed because of foul weather. From then until 15 November, when they were relieved by 2nd South Wales Borderers, the Rifles spent time in a very wet camp in Trônes Wood, in billets or in the line where they endured further heavy shelling in trenches that the Germans had 'marked to an inch'. On the morning of 19 November the battalion said goodbye to the Somme and entrained at Dernancourt.

The Somme campaign was drawing to a close and it was finally decided to end operations during the battle of the Ancre, which opened on 13 November and concluded on the 18th.

During this final phase of the campaign two more Irishmen earned the Victoria Cross. On 4 October Second Lieutenant Henry Kelly, 10th Duke of Wellington's Regiment, whose parent formation, 69 Brigade of 23rd Division, was also involved in the battle for le Transloy, was the first. The Germans held the village of le Sars and two understrength companies of Kelly's battalion were ordered to attack it. The attack, across a hundred yards of muddy ground under heavy rifle and machine-gun fire, was stalled by barbed wire that had not been cut by the artillery. Two officers were killed at the wire and the attack might have failed had it not been for Kelly. His VC citation reads:

> For most conspicuous bravery in an attack. He twice rallied his company under the heaviest fire, and finally led the only three available men into the enemy trench, and there remained bombing until two of them had become casualties and enemy reinforcements had arrived. He then carried his Company Sergeant Major, who had been wounded, back to our trenches, a distance of 70 yards, and subsequently three other soldiers. He set a fine example of gallantry and endurance.

Kelly later earned the Military Cross and Bar in Italy and was also awarded the Belgian *Croix de Guerre* and the French *Médaille Militaire*. Born in Manchester, the son of a native of Sandyford, County Dublin,[16] Kelly later served in the new Irish National Army during the civil war that followed the establishment of the Irish Free State; he served again in the British Army during the Second World War.

---

[16] His mother's maiden name was McGarry.

The final Irish Victoria Cross of the Somme campaign was awarded to Sergeant Robert Downie of 2nd Royal Dublin Fusiliers, the Old Toughs. Although born in Glasgow, Downie had Irish parents, both natives of Dublin, and when he joined the Army in 1912 he enlisted in the Royal Dublin Fusiliers rather than a Scottish regiment. Downie's valour was also demonstrated during the Transloy battle. His battalion was part of 10 Brigade, alongside 1st Royal Irish Fusiliers, and by nightfall on 23 October the Old Toughs had captured German gun positions east of Lesboeufs and a strongpoint beyond the positions. Downie had played a critical part in the battalion's success, as his VC citation records:

> When most of the officers had become casualties, this non-commissioned officer, utterly regardless of personal danger, moved about under heavy fire and reorganised the attack, which had been temporarily checked. At the critical moment he rushed forward alone, shouting: 'Come on, the Dubs!' This stirring appeal met with immediate response, and the line rushed forward at his call.

Although wounded early in the attack, Robert Downie had continued to lead his company and he captured a German machine gun, killing the crew. This inspiring leadership led to the fall of a position that had already repelled four or five British attacks. Downie also earned the Military Medal, as did one of his brothers, was Mentioned in Despatches twice and was wounded five times.

Also involved in those final battles were 2nd Royal Inniskilling and 10th Royal Dublin Fusiliers. The former battalion was a veteran of the Somme, having taken part in the attacks on 1 July, but the latter was going into action on the Western Front for the first time. The Dublins were serving in 190 Brigade of an unusual formation, 63rd (Royal Naval) Division,[17] which had served in Gallipoli before being transferred to France, where the Dublins joined it on 19 August, having also just arrived in the country.

Meanwhile, 2nd Inniskillings had spent some days in close support of 117 and 56 Brigades at St Pierre Divion before being relieved by 7th Worcesters and rejoining their parent 96 Brigade at Mailly Maillet where they spent the night of 17/18 November. On the 18th the battalion moved into the

---

[17] The Royal Naval Division, as it had been known earlier, had been under Admiralty command and included sailors assigned to military duties and Royal Marines. After Gallipoli the division had come under War Office control and was assigned the number of the disbanded 63rd (2nd Northumbrian) Division of the Territorial Force.

front line near Beaumont Hamel to relieve 16th Highland Light Infantry and remained there until the 24th. On the day before its relief by 1st South Staffords, a party of eighty men under Captain S. E. Clarke was detailed to join three companies of 16th Lancashire Fusiliers in an attack, or raid, on Munich Trench with the task of locating and bringing back a party of infantry from 91 Brigade who were cut off in dug-outs near there. The attack began at 3.30pm and, although the attackers reached and entered Munich Trench, where there was some desperate close-quarter fighting, they were unable to achieve the second objective and locate the missing troops. Inniskilling casualties in this action included five killed, forty-five wounded, including Captain Clarke, and seventeen missing. During their time in the front-line trenches, battalion casualties, excluding those in the raid, were seven dead, including a subaltern who died of his wounds, forty-one wounded and five missing. As weather conditions were worsening, and the battle was closed down on the 19th, their relief on the 24th ended 2nd Inniskillings' fighting experiences on the Somme in 1916.

The Royal Naval Division had its baptism of fire on the Somme on 13 November, an operation in which the Dublins took part. Since this was the division's first action on the Western Front, the planning was more detailed and careful than usual and all moves were explained carefully. Advancing along the Ancre, the division was to capture Beaucourt. It had four objectives: the first was the 'Dotted Green line', the German front-line trench system, followed by the 'Green Line', the road to Beaucourt station, which ran along a ridge that the Germans had fortified. The third objective, the 'Yellow Line', was a trench beyond that road which lay around the south-west edge of what was left of Beaucourt. On the final objective, the 'Red Line', 63rd Division was to consolidate.

In the first phase of the attack several critical points were taken but every company commander in 1st Royal Marine Light Infantry was killed before the first objective was reached. The plan had been to leap-frog battalions to the final objective but some 50 per cent of the attackers had become casualties in the attack on the 'Dotted Green Line'. 'Leap-frogging' became impossible when it was discovered that the German trenches had been damaged so badly by the preparatory bombardment that men were becoming disoriented. Realising this, Lieutenant Colonel Bernard Freyberg, commanding Hood Battalion, decided to press on and it was due to his drive and initiative that the 'Yellow Line' was reached and Beaucourt was taken. Freyberg was wounded four times and was awarded the Victoria Cross.[18]

After getting into the German first line, 10th Dublins were also held up. However, the following day the battalion, with the support of two tanks from Auchonvillers, was able to resume the advance. Although the tanks became bogged down in the muddy, chalky ground they were still able to fire their 6-pounder guns at the German trenches. This close fire support allowed the Dublins to surge forward into the trenches, overpower the defenders and take prisoner some 400 German soldiers. 'Muddy ground' does not adequately describe the conditions in which this battle was fought: the Dublins', 'a battalion of shopkeepers', advance to the German trenches was made in a near blizzard that turned to sleet before falling as rain.

By the end of the operation, the objectives had been taken, including Beaumont Hamel, from which the German defenders had inflicted such hurt on 36th (Ulster) Division soldiers on 1 July.

On 19 November 4th Canadian Division launched another attack in which some 1,250 men were lost while 19th Division lost some units in a blizzard. They were never seen again. Although Hubert Gough, commanding Fifth Army, the former Reserve Army,[19] was still optimistic and asked Haig for 'one more go', the Commander-in-Chief decided to close down operations. Gough's optimism had been based on aerial reconnaissance reports indicating that the Germans were pulling out of their positions. However, ground patrols discovered that the reverse was true: the Germans were determined to hold on for the time being. Nor were the French happy with Haig's decision. They felt let down by their ally and considered that a decisive victory would have been the result 'if the British had persevered'.

Haig's decision was based on the vital necessity to rest his soldiers, to allow the divisions to absorb and train drafts of fresh soldiers and to train as formations for future operations. Under his command in 1916 Haig had fifty-six British, Dominion or Imperial divisions, of which fifty-three had been engaged at some point in the Somme battles.

---

[18] During the war he was also awarded the DSO three times and became the youngest general in the Army.
[19] The title Fifth Army was adopted from 30 October 1916.

MG 08 machine gun

The MG 08, *Maschinengewehr 08*, an adaptation of Hiram Maxim's original 1884 Maxim gun, was the German Army's standard machine gun during the First World War. Produced in several variants, the weapon later saw limited service as a heavy machine gun in the Second World War. It was also referred to as the Spandau 08 since some were manufactured in the government arsenal at Spandau, as well as by DWM (*Deutsche Waffen und Munitionsfabriken*) in Berlin.

Developed from the licence-made MG 01, the MG 08 was adopted in 1908 – hence the 08 designation – and was a water-cooled weapon, in common with its British 'cousin', the Vickers. As with the latter, the MG 08 fired belted ammunition, using 250-round belts of 7.92mm bullets. Depending on the lock assembly the firing rate was either 500 or 600 rounds per minute, although sustained firing led to overheating.

In German service the MG 08 was usually mounted on a sled, or *Schlittenlafette*, that could be dragged, shoulder carried or moved on a cart. Alternatively a tripod mount could be fitted, as in the Turkish army. The effective range of the MG 08 was about 2,200 yards (2,000m) but it could fire up to a distance of 3,900 yards (3,600m), significantly more than two miles, in the indirect fire role, using a separate sight with a range calculator. In the indirect fire role

the MG 08 could operate from cover, adding to its effectiveness on the battlefield.

Some 12,000 MG 08s were in service with the German army in August 1914. Manufacture increased from 200 per month to 3,000 per month by 1916, later rising to over 14,000 per month. A brutally effective battlefield weapon, the MG 08 that dominated no man's land on the Western Front and caused many deaths in the Entente armies.

A lighter and more easily transported version, the MG 08/15, was developed in 1915 but did not come into service until 1917. The MG 08 was also adapted for use in aircraft as the IMG 08 and the LMG 08/15, and continued in use in the Chinese Army until the 1960s.

MG 08 MACHINE GUN	
Designed	1908
Weight	65 kg – 69 kg (with water)
Length	1175 mm
Diameter	70 mm
Firing range	2000 m (effective)
	3600 m (maximum)
Firing rate	500–600 rounds/minute
Ammunition	250-round belt
Crew	four

Somme 1916

The battle honour *Somme 1916* was awarded to these Irish regiments.

Further battle honours for the engagements of the Somme campaign were awarded: Albert 1916, Bazentin, Delville Wood, Pozières, Guillemont, Ginchy, Flers-Courcelette, Morval, Thiepval, le Transloy, Ancre Heights and Ancre 1916.

Every honour approved for the campaign, except Thiepval, was awarded to at least one Irish regiment. Thirteen Irish regiments, plus a Territorial Force battalion recruited from London's Irish community fought on the Somme, as did four battalions of Northumberland Fusiliers, partly recruited from the Irish community on Tyneside and known as the Tyneside Irish. Over 40 Irish units were involved, including 35 line infantry battalions, both battalions of the Irish Guards, three regular cavalry regiments and both Special Reserve cavalry regiments.

SOMME 1916
ALBERT 1916
BAZENTIN
DELVILLE WOOD
POZIÈRES
GUILLEMONT
GINCHY
FLERS-COURCELETTE
MORVAL
THIEPVAL
LE TRANSLOY
ANCRE HEIGHTS
ANCRE 1916

4TH (ROYAL IRISH) DRAGOON GUARDS

NORTH IRISH HORSE

ROYAL IRISH REGIMENT

PRINCESS VICTORIA'S (ROYAL IRISH FUSILIERS)

ROYAL MUNSTER FUSILIERS

6TH (INNISKILLING) DRAGOONS

SOUTH IRISH HORSE

ROYAL INNISKILLING FUSILIERS

CONNAUGHT RANGERS

ROYAL DUBLIN FUSILIERS

103 (TYNESIDE IRISH) BRIGADE

8TH (THE KING'S ROYAL IRISH) HUSSARS

IRISH GUARDS

ROYAL IRISH RIFLES

PRINCE OF WALES'S LEINSTER REGIMENT (ROYAL CANADIANS)

18TH (COUNTY OF LONDON) BATTALION THE LONDON REGIMENT (LONDON IRISH RIFLES)

There was no doubt that all those divisions were battle-weary and in need of rest. The terrain was also a major factor in Haig's decision. In his own words:

> The ground, sodden and broken by countless shell-holes, can only be described as a morass, in places bottomless. Between the lines and behind, in many places, it is almost impassable. The supply of food and ammunition is carried out with the greatest difficulty and immense labour, by men so worn out by this and trench maintenance that frequent reliefs are unavoidable.

In areas where wheeled vehicles could not operate it often took four men to carry a stretcher, over distances as great as 3,000 yards. Both patients and stretcher-bearers were often at risk from shell-fire and even from machine-gun bullets, as the German MG 08 machine gun had an extreme range of almost 4,000 yards. Then there were the health problems, which were endemic in trench warfare. Men fell ill from diseases such as dysentery and measles while trench foot, frostbite and renal inflammation also took their toll to such an extent that casualties from illness exceeded those from battle by some 3 per cent.

Total British casualties in the Somme campaign exceeded 450,000, to which may be added about 200,000 French (not including those at Verdun). German casualties exceeded 600,000 – of 800,000 on all fronts during 1916.

8 The Results

As winter set in the planners' thoughts turned to 1917 and the renewal of the offensive on the Western Front, but for the soldier on the ground there remained the reality of day-to-day life and the memory of lost comrades. Some of that reality was reflected in the disbandment or amalgamation of service, or war-raised, battalions: 8th Royal Munster Fusiliers, reduced to fewer than 500 personnel, disbanded on 26 November, the personnel moving to the 1st Battalion which transferred from 48 to 47 Brigade. A month earlier, on 25 October, 49 Brigade's two Irish Fusilier battalions had amalgamated as 7th/8th Royal Irish Fusiliers, reducing the brigade to three battalions, a shortfall made up by the transfer of 2nd Royal Irish from 22 Brigade in 7th Division. On 11 November 2nd Royal Dublin Fusiliers also joined 16th (Irish) Division, quitting 10 Brigade of 4th Division for 48 Brigade.

Following its actions at Guillemont and Ginchy 16th (Irish) Division left the Somme area and Fourth Army for Flanders where it joined General Plumer's Second Army, which already included 36th (Ulster) Division. The latter formation had been rebuilding its strength since its experiences of 1 July. That rebuilding also changed the character of the division since many of the reinforcements drafted in to replace the casualties were not from any part of Ireland and many were Catholic to boot. In the same fashion, the original complexion of 16th Division had changed dramatically. It is worth recording the total number of fatalities sustained by each during 1916: 16th (Irish) Division lost 2,663 dead, of whom 1,167 perished on the Somme and the remainder at Loos, while 36th (Ulster) Division lost 1,944 on the Somme. Their combined Somme death toll of 3,111 is raised to close to 4,000 by the deaths in all Irish units during the campaign.

The *Official History* notes that 'For this disastrous loss of the finest manhood of the United Kingdom and Ireland there was only a small gain of ground to show'. Was Edmonds, the official historian, correct in this comment? When German sources are examined, and the reaction of the German high command taken into account, it becomes clear that Edmonds was mistaken. The German equivalent of the *Official History* tells a different story with its record of 'the great losses of [1916]' which totalled 1.4 million, with 800,000 of those in the period from July to October inclusive on all fronts, of which about 75 per cent occurred on the Somme. At regimental level, German histories note the exceptionally heavy casualties suffered, with a spell in the trenches reducing companies to as few as two dozen men, while battalions might muster only 160. The effect of such losses was debilitating on morale and effectiveness and many German writers agree that the losses of their armies on the Somme meant that they never recovered fully their levels of professionalism and effectiveness.

Ludendorff accepted that the September battles were 'among the most fiercely contested of the whole war, and far exceeded all previous offensives as regards the number of men and the amount of material employed'. He admitted that the Franco-British attacks in the Battle of Morval, 25–28 September, were 'the heaviest of the many heavy engagements' in the Somme campaign. Another German commander, Crown Prince Rupprecht of Bavaria, wrote that 'September brought the heaviest losses of the whole battle' and went on to comment that 'what remained of the first-class peace-trained German infantry had been expended' by the end of November. This assessment reflects a remarkable, but little appreciated, truth: that one of the world's most professional and best trained armies had been attacked and badly beaten by what German generals had considered to be no more than an amateur army, an imperial *gendarmerie*, led by generals of no great quality. The German *Großer Generalstab* (Great General Staff) would learn as the war progressed that they had underestimated hugely the contemptibly small British Army and its commanders, especially when that Army provided the dynamo for the Entente armies that brought Germany to defeat in 1918. However, in November 1916, the German armies still possessed the physical strength, determination and resilience to ride out the storm.

Nonetheless, the new German commanders, von Hindenburg and Ludendorff, who had replaced Falkenhayn and his team in August, had been taken by surprise by the operational situation on the Western Front with Hindenburg describing it as 'an evil inheritance'. They had decided that the German forces in the Verdun sector would go on the defensive while formations from that sector would relieve some of those on the Somme which, in turn, would move to Verdun. Falkenhayn was sent to the East to counter the new threat from Romania, taking with him some divisions from the West. Meanwhile the Brusilov Offensive continued on the Eastern Front.

Hindenburg and Ludendorff were especially critical of the tactics underlying the defence on the Somme. The new tactics introduced in July of holding ground at all costs and counter-attacking every Franco-British success had led only to more casualties. In fact, it had played into the hands of the Entente commanders, and allowed the adoption of a policy that has sometimes been described as 'offence by defence' – seizing a piece of ground from the Germans and then waiting for the counter-attack and the opportunity to inflict severe losses from heavy fire on the attackers. This developed into an operational tactic known as *grignotage* to the French or 'bite and hold' to the British.

Ludendorff instituted a new form of more flexible defence that was 'broader and looser and better adapted to the ground'. Thus the defence could absorb the energy of attacks without throwing away the lives of the defenders. Defensive positions were to be deeper and the previous reliance on fixed, heavily-fortified strongpoints and dug-outs was to give way to a system that included an outpost line that could be given up, allowing the attackers into a zone commanded by strongpoints and machine-gun posts, the fire from which would break up the attacks. Firepower was to be more important than manpower and the German armies paid their foes the compliment of adopting their practices by re-equipping infantry units with trench mortars, light machine guns and grenade launchers. Whereas the German infantry units had hitherto placed considerable reliance on the hand grenade, Ludendorff decreed that the rifle should be restored to its earlier primacy as the infantryman's principal weapon, thus enabling units to engage attackers at greater distances and prevent them entering German lines to engage the defenders in costly close-quarter fights in the trenches.

With artillery and air reinforcements, and a revised artillery doctrine that allowed divisional commanders to co-ordinate their artillery support, the

German commanders hoped to create a more flexible and speedier response to attacks. A new command structure was also introduced with three army groups being created, with Crown Prince Rupprecht appointed to command the Northern Army Group, in the Somme sector, with the rank of field marshal.

All of these changes signalled one inescapable fact: Germany had lost the initiative. While the high command and the politicians studied the strategic situation, it was hoped that Germany's armies could hold on until winter set in, which would permit a re-organisation of her forces to make them more effective, and allow them to fight on into 1917. The Entente remained superior in both manpower and *matériel* and Germany would have to find ways of countering those advantages. In the meantime, engineers were working on a new defensive system. The decision to build this had been taken in September 1916 and the intention was that the armies could make a strategic retreat to this system when it was complete. The new system, the *Siegfriedstellung*, or Hindenburg Line, was to be a deep defence, laid out according to the new principles, and was to be built during the winter. No longer did the German armies possess sufficient reserves to allow them to endure another campaign of attrition on the length of front held in 1916; Joffre's plan to wear down Germany's armies in the west had succeeded. The *Siegfriedstellung* would reduce the length of front to be defended. Once the decision to build it had been taken, it was critical that the existing front be held and so divisions were deployed from elsewhere on the Western Front to enable this to happen. The tenacious defence by German divisions in the later battles along the Somme is evidence of the determination to hold on until winter, allowing the new defences to be completed. Interestingly, although the Germans noted the British introduction of tanks, they made little effort to produce a similar weapon. They were quick to appreciate that the tanks were vulnerable to fire from field guns, which were pressed into service as anti-tank weapons. However, this was a tactical innovation and not something decreed by the *Großer Generalstab* although it did approve the development of dedicated anti-tank weapons. It never showed any enthusiasm for tanks and only one German tank, the cumbersome A7V, made a battlefield appearance. Only twenty A7Vs were produced, although Germany did field some thirty captured British tanks.

In February 1917 the German armies withdrew to the *Siegfriedstellung*. The map on pp 90/91 shows that the ground thus conceded to the Entente

Eric N. F. Bell VC
9th Battalion
Royal Inniskilling Fusiliers

Geoffrey St G. S. Cather VC
9th Battalion
Royal Irish Fusiliers

Robert Downie VC
2nd Battalion
Royal Dublin Fusiliers

Victoria Cross

The highest gallantry award for servicemen in the UK, Commonwealth or Imperial forces, the Victoria Cross was awarded to ten Irish soldiers during the Somme campaign. On 1 July 1916 four members of 36th (Ulster) Division earned the VC; three were posthumous awards. Two VCs went to members of 16th (Irish) Division at Guillemont on 3 September; both survived. Of the other four VC laureates on the Somme, one was an Irishman in the Australian Imperial Force, two were in English regiments and the other was the Glasgow-born son of Dublin parents in an Irish regiment. The commanding officer of 8th Gloucestershire Regiment, Adrian Carton de Wiart, earned the VC at la Boiselle on 2/3 July 1916. Brussels-born, Carton de Wiart had an Irish grandmother, considered himself Irish, settled in County Cork and died there in 1963.

Frederick J. Edwards VC
12th Battalion
The Middlesex Regiment

John V. Holland VC
3rd Battalion, Prince of Wales's
Leinster Regiment

Thomas Hughes VC
6th Battalion
Connaught Rangers

Henry Kelly VC
Duke of Wellington's
(West Riding) Regiment

William F. McFadzean VC
14th Battalion
Royal Irish Rifles

Martin O'Meara VC
16th Battalion, Australian
Imperial Force

Robert Quigg VC
12th Battalion
Royal Irish Rifles

was far from the 'small gain' to which Edmonds referred. Strategically, that German withdrawal had another, and greater, significance. In March 1918, with Russia out of the war, the Germans transferred armies to the west and launched a major offensive that fell upon the British and French armies along the Somme. Before long they regained the ground they had given up but their advance was fought to a standstill without achieving its objectives, one of which was to cut off the BEF from the Channel ports. Had the German armies been able to launch the 1918 spring offensive from the lines they had held in 1916, and with troops of the quality they had lost on the Somme that year, that offensive would have been much more dangerous and they might have been able to force the Entente powers to the negotiating table. Thus it may be argued that the sacrifices made by the BEF on the Somme in 1916 helped ensure the final victory in 1918.

9 Aftermath

In Ireland the Somme campaign left many homes bereaved of a husband and father or of sons. However, it took some time before the true nature and extent of 36th (Ulster) Division's losses on 1 July became known to the families, friends and neighbours of the casualties. The *Londonderry Sentinel*, then a twice-weekly publication, published an extensive casualty list on the 8th and was still publishing casualty lists from 1 July at the beginning of August. Earlier headlines had included such optimistic claims as: BATTLE OF THE SOMME: ALL STILL GOING WELL, with, in smaller print, 'Further Progress on British Front'.

James Conaghan was a 14-year-old boy in the Waterside area of Londonderry, living close to the city's Ebrington Barracks. He died in 1980 at the age of 79 but had never been able to forget the aftermath of the opening of the Somme campaign. The quiet little streets of his neighbourhood were stricken by the grief of wide-scale loss and he recalled the frequent appearance of the Post Office messenger bearing the telegrams that told of death, injury or 'missing in action'. Few homes were spared the visit and grief overwhelmed the womenfolk of the surrounding streets as they learned of the deaths of husbands, fathers, sons, brothers or boyfriends. 'The women were out in the streets, screaming and crying. Some homes had lost more than one man. It was just … terrible on them,' he remembered. Many Army families lived in the area close to the barracks and there were also many families of young, and not-so-young, men who had joined either the Irish or Ulster Volunteers and then enlisted in the new battalions of the Irish regiments. All found themselves bound together in the greatest communal tragedy their city had suffered for generations.

That sense of grief was widespread. In the Ulster counties it was felt most acutely in the days following the opening assault on the Somme. We have already noted Bob Grange's memory of how his home town of Ballyclare was affected. Similar experiences were felt across towns and villages whose menfolk had taken part in that assault. But it did not end there. Soldiers from across the island were involved in almost all the battles of the Somme campaign and many lost their lives. When 16th (Irish) Division went into action at Guillemont and Ginchy in September the story of pain and loss was repeated. To many homes in west Belfast came the news that a loved one had been killed or wounded while, on 22 September, Private James McCann of 6th Connaught Rangers, a Belfast man, died of wounds that had caused him to be evacuated to Britain for treatment. For the families of soldiers of 16th Division the litany of names of the dead and wounded had been a continuing one since early in the year with the division's losses at Loos being added to by those on the Somme.

At the same time the Somme campaign was passing into history and myth. Within days of the repulse of 36th (Ulster) Division's assault a different version of what had happened was passing into popular belief. This was the result of a series of letters from soldiers and officers, one of whom was a staff officer at divisional HQ, Captain Wilfred B. Spender. Some of Spender's letters to his wife and others included injudicious and quite personal remarks about individuals and when one was published in a newspaper there were concerns that others might follow. In a letter to his wife, written on 2 July, Spender laid the foundation for the myth that 29th and 32nd Divisions had let the Ulster Division down. He wrote that:

> The enemy's first, second and third lines were soon taken, and still the waves of men went on, getting thinner and thinner but without hesitation. The enemy's fourth line fell before these men who would not be stopped. I saw parties of them, now much reduced indeed, enter the fifth line of the enemy's trenches, our final objective. It could not be held as the Division had advanced into a narrow salient. The Corps on our right and left had been unable to advance so that the Ulstermen were the target of the concentrated hostile guns and machine guns behind and on both flanks, though the enemy in front were vanquished and retiring. The order to retire was given, but many parties preferred to die in the ground they had won so hardly.

In her response (which was dated 4 July, which says much for the efficiency of the postal service) his wife added another layer to that foundation with the comment:

> It must have nearly broken your heart to watch such things, but oh how proud I am. I can't write about it. My heart is too full. It seems so cruel a thing to have happened that the flanking Div[ision]s should have failed to come up.

Of course, the other divisions had not failed to come up. They had tried manfully to advance but had been stopped in their tracks by machine guns and shells, paying a terrible price for their courage.

Spender's response to his wife's letter was written on the 6th. Once again it included remarks that ought not to have been committed to paper:

> Our men are quite cheery and saying they don't want any Derby recruits. The General [Nugent] wrote an excellent order of the day and made a very nice speech to all the brigades, nearly breaking down. Somehow he fails to strike the spark, so the officers say, tho' it is absolutely genuine. I think he cannot quite forgive himself.

This was also the letter in which he referred to Captain Davidson of 13th Rifles having been killed 'after earning the VC'. In his letter of the 2nd he had commented on the courage of the Ulster Division's soldiers and on how they had performed:

> The Ulster Division has lost more than half the men who attacked, and in doing so has sacrificed itself for the Empire which has treated them none too well. The much derided Ulster Volunteer Force has won a name which equals any in History. Their devotion, which no doubt has helped the advance elsewhere, deserves the gratitude of the British Empire. It is due to the memory of these brave heroes that their beloved Province shall be fairly treated.

On 10 July a letter appeared in the *Belfast News Letter*. Written by Lance Corporal William Greer to his parents, who lived at Stranmillis, it told one man's story of Z Day and must also have played a part in creating the popular image of the Ulster Division's sacrifice on the Somme. Describing how the division, which had been holding the lines on the Somme since they 'came out', 'has made a name for itself these past few days', he noted that they had been ordered to take, 'if possible', four lines of German trenches.

The German lines were bombarded for almost a week before we went over the parapet. On 1st July the boys were all very cool about matters, but we had to face a very heavy fire from machine guns, though our artillery had accounted for a big lot of them in the bombardment. We reached the first line of the trenches alright and pushed on to the second and third without meeting very much resistance, as any Germans who survived the preliminary bombardment were almost demoralised by the shellfire. We held on to the four lines of trenches until nightfall, we had to temporarily fall back to our lines owing to our right and left flanks not being able to push forward with our Division at the time. However, they were regained later, and, as I write, we still hold them – not our Division, of course, but another relieving one. The bombardment just before we attacked was terrible. It developed in intensity an hour before the infantry started operations, and how any living being in the German lines could survive it is a mystery.

Such were the losses of the Ulster Division that the annual Twelfth of July celebrations were cancelled by the Grand Orange Lodge of Ireland. There was nothing to celebrate. In time, however, the perceived first day of the Somme campaign would take its own place in the Orange calendar, with marches and wreathlaying ceremonies marking the heroic sacrifice of the men who had died in France, a blood sacrifice that, as Professor Keith Jeffery has so succinctly described, marked 'the Union sealed in blood', a sacrifice that paralleled the blood sacrifice of those who had died in Dublin in April in rebellion against the Union.

As the years passed the perception of the nature of that sacrifice has changed. It was not to be seen as heroic failure but as a shining example of courage, endeavour and success in the midst of tragic failure. Today there is a common belief that the Ulster Division was the sole British division to take and hold its objectives that grim July day a century ago. As the reader will have gleaned from the preceding chapters, this was not so. In fact, 36th (Ulster) Division succeeded only in penetrating some of its objectives. It fought desperately in the Schwaben Redoubt but did not hold it; the redoubt was recaptured by the German defenders. The simple test of whether an operation has succeeded is that the ground attacked is still in the attackers' possession the next day. On 2 July 1916 German troops held the Schwaben Redoubt, just as they had twenty-four hours earlier.

In contrast, on the morning of 2 July the Germans no longer held many of the positions that had been assaulted by divisions from XV and XIII

Corps. In the former corps' sector we have seen that the villages of Mametz and Fricourt were taken, the latter being surrounded on the 1st and taken on the 2nd. XV Corps' operations involved 2nd Royal Irish in 22 Brigade of 7th Division. In XIII Corps' sector, the extreme right of the British line, there was also success with objectives being taken and held. Although no Irish battalions were involved in these operations, 18th (Eastern) Division's infantry could attribute their remarkable success to two factors: their outstanding GOC, Major General Ivor Maxse, who had trained the division to a very high level of effectiveness, and the artillery support from their own guns, using a fireplan devised by Major Alan Brooke, a Fermanagh man. Brooke's use of the more sophisticated rolling bombardment devised by the French artillery, helped to ensure that Maxse's infantry were 'shot' on to their objectives; to their right 30th Division took Montauban. Elements of the same French practice were also clear in XV Corps. It is a pity that the achievements of XV and XIII Corps on the British right and Fayolle's French troops to their right have never received the attention they deserve while Brooke has been all but forgotten in the popular story of the Somme, although his achievements have rightly been recognised by military men and especially Gunners.

The emphasis on the courageous sacrifice of 36th (Ulster) Division has also meant that the achievements and sufferings of 16th (Irish) Division and other Irish units in the campaign have been side-lined. We have noted the losses suffered by Hickie's division at Guillemont and Ginchy, which rank with those of Nugent's men: 16th Division had already been weakened by attrition when it went into action. Elsewhere on 1 July and throughout the campaign other Irish units fought valiantly but their contribution has received less notice than is deserved. In particular, it is sad to read claims that the flanking divisions 'failed' to advance and therefore left the Ulster Division exposed in a salient. Those flanking divisions suffered heavily in their efforts to get forward, with losses of 5,240 in 29th Division – higher than in 36th Division – and 3,949 in 32nd Division. Both flanking divisions included regular battalions of Royal Inniskilling Fusiliers and 1st Inniskillings of 29th Division suffered more casualties, 568 in total, than all but two of the Ulster Division battalions (12th Rifles and 11th Inniskillings with 595 and 589 respectively). With five battalions committed to the attack on Z Day, the Inniskillings suffered over 2,200 casualties.

It is a common perception across Ireland and farther afield that those Irish soldiers who came home on demobilisation in 1919 and later to what is now the Republic of Ireland found a hostile environment in which it was considered unsafe to proclaim an identity as a former 'British soldier'. While there is an element of truth in this, the myth that Ireland forgot completely her soldier sons who fought in khaki between 1914 and 1919 is simply that – a myth. The government of the new Saorstát Éireann did not acknowledge the service and sacrifice of Irish soldiers in what was then called the Great War and it also created an 'official' version of recent Irish history in which the patriots were those who had taken up arms against the United Kingdom in 1916 and from 1919 to 1921. Thus generations of schoolchildren in the new state grew up knowing little of the part played by their ancestors in the First World War. More recently we have been told that the memory of that generation has only been discovered since the 'peace process' in Northern Ireland began in 1994 and especially since the Belfast Agreement of 1998.

This ignores another truth. While a state may try to write history to suit its own purposes, it is impossible to obliterate from the memory of individual human beings the stories of members of their own families. Thus for generations the memory of men who died on the Western Front and in other theatres of war remained alive in their families, especially in the hearts and minds of those who remembered those men. That memory was handed down to later generations and there were very many homes throughout Ireland where, for example, prints of Fortunino Matania's painting of Father Gleeson's Last Absolution of the Munsters at Rue du Bois in 1915 hung, often alongside photographs of family members who had made the supreme sacrifice. Catholic families treasured 'In Memoriam' cards for men who had died and it was noticeable just how many of those had survived when groups such as the Royal Munster Fusiliers and Royal Dublin Fusiliers Associations were established in the 1990s.

There is another very strong piece of evidence that indicates that 'national amnesia' did not set in in 1922 as is so often suggested. The British Legion established branches in the Free State almost as soon as it was created in 1921. With the War of Independence still underway, followed upon the creation of the Saorstát by civil war, it was 1924 before any commemoration of the Armistice could be organised. The first such commemoration took place in Dublin's College Green on 11 November 1924, the first year of full peace in Ireland. If the myth of national amnesia was true this would have seen a small turnout. Instead some 20,000 ex-servicemen observed the two-minute silence, as did another 50,000 people. Moreover, the collection for the Haig Fund through the sale of poppies in Dublin was higher than that in Belfast and remained so for almost a decade until the economy of the new state was brought low by the international recession.

A focal point of that commemoration was the Ginchy Cross, made in France to General Hickie's design, to commemorate the dead of 16th (Irish) Division in the Somme campaign. Some years later, at the suggestion of the Irish government, the commemoration was moved to the Phoenix Park. There was no official representation at this ceremony but the Irish government did observe the occasion through its representatives in other Commonwealth countries and did so in London until Ireland's withdrawal from the Commonwealth. The Ginchy Cross is now preserved in the National War Memorial Gardens at Islandbridge, itself another piece of evidence that the men of 1914–19 were not forgotten. The gardens were created before the Second World War and built by labour drawn equally from veterans of the UK forces and the new Irish Defence Forces. An official opening was to have been held on 11 November 1939 but another world war intervened, leaving an unanswered question: would Eamon de Valera, an Taoiseach, have attended?

There is no doubt that the 'troubles' which beset Northern Ireland from 1969 onwards had an influence on attitudes to those Irishmen who fought in both world wars, but it is wrong to project the attitudes of the years from 1969 to 1998 onto the past. It is interesting to note that the Remembrance Sunday parade in Limerick was the largest in Ireland before 1969 and, according to the Limerick Branch of the Royal British Legion, probably holds that distinction again today.

Over 40,000 Irishmen, and some women, perished in the First World War. The losses of the Somme were horrendous but there had also been great losses in 1914 and 1915 and again in 1917 and 1918 – indeed the advance to victory in 1918 brought a death rate that was every bit as bad as those of the years of trench warfare. Those Irish who volunteered to fight for the 'freedom of small nations' a century ago deserve their place in history as much as any others. To paraphrase the Kohima Memorial of 1944, they gave their today for our tomorrow.

Bibliographical Note

Primary sources

These include the war diaries of the Irish divisions, brigades and battalions that fought in the Somme campaign, which are to be found in the series WO95 in the UK National Archives, Kew, Richmond, Surrey. While such diaries can vary in the amount of detail contained in them they generally provide a good picture of the activities of the formation or unit concerned and are invaluable in the quest to create the broadest possible account of the involvement of those bodies on the Somme. Also in the series WO95 are the war diaries of the many combat support and combat service support units that played critical parts in the campaign, such as the various arms of the Royal Regiment of Artillery, the Corps of Royal Engineers, the Army Chaplains Department, Army Service Corps, Royal Army Medical Corps and the Royal Flying Corps. More recently the war diaries for 1 July 1916, most of which are digitised and downloadable from the National Archives website (www.nationalarchives.gov.uk), have also been published by Pen and Sword Books of Barnsley as *Slaughter on the Somme, 1 July 1916: The Complete War Diaries Of the British Army's Worst Day*, edited by Martin Mace and John Grehan. Jack Sheldon's *The German Army on the Somme 1914–1916* is the best English language source for the German army's experience of the Somme campaign.

Although it has been fashionable in some circles to criticise the official history of the First World War, these volumes (of which there are over a hundred) remain an accurate guide to the ebb and flow of the war and especially that of the Somme campaign, which is covered in *France and Belgium 1916*, the fifth part of the series, of which there are two volumes: Brigadier General Edmonds' *Sir Douglas Haig's Command to the 1st July: Battle of the Somme* (HMSO, 1932) and Captain Wilfred Miles' *2 July 1916 to the End of the Battle of the Somme* (Macmillan & Co., 1938).

Secondary Sources

Adkin, Mark, *The Western Front Companion: The Complete Guide to How the Armies Fought for Four Devastating Years, 1914–1918* (Aurum Press, London, 2013)

Bredin, Brigadier A. E. C., DSO MC DL, *A History of the Irish Soldier* (Century Books, Belfast, 1987)

Denman, Terence, *Ireland's Unknown Soldiers: The 16th (Irish) Division in the Great War* (Irish Academic Press, Dublin, 1992)

Doherty, Richard, and Truesdale, David, *Irish Winners of the Victoria Cross* (Four Courts Press, Dublin, 2000)

Falls, Cyril, *History of the Ulster Division* (McCaw, Stevenson & Orr, Belfast, 1922)

Farndale, General Sir Martin, KCB, *History of the Royal Regiment of Artillery: Western Front 1914–18* (The Royal Artillery Institution, London, 1986)

Gleichen, Major General Lord Edward, KCVO CB CMG DSO, *Chronology of the Great War* (Constable & Co., London, 1918 to 1920; re-published in one volume by Greenhill Books, London, 1988)

Griffith, Paddy, *The Great War on the Western Front: A Short History* (Pen & Sword Books, Barnsley, 2008)

Harris, H. E. D., *The Irish Regiments in the First World War* (Mercier Press, Cork, 1968)

Jeffery, Keith, *1916: A Global History* (Bloomsbury, London, 2015)

Johnstone, Tom, *Orange Green & Khaki: The Story of the Irish Regiments in the Great War, 1914–18* (Gill and Macmillan, Dublin, 1992)

Liddle, Peter H., *The 1916 Battle of the Somme: A Reappraisal* (Leo Cooper, London, 1992)

MacDonagh, Michael, *The Irish on the Somme* (Hodder and Stoughton, London, 1917)

Middlebrook, Martin, *The First Day on the Somme* (Allen Lane, London, 1971)

Myatt, Frederick, *The British Infantry 1660–1945: The Evolution of a Fighting Force* (Blandford Press, Poole, 1983)

Philpott, William, *Bloody Victory: The Sacrifice on the Somme and the Making of the Twentieth Century* (Little, Brown, London, 2009)

  Attrition: Fighting the First World War (Little, Brown, London, 2014)

Sheffield, Gary, *A Short History of the First World War* (Oneworld Publications, London, 2014)

Sheldon, Jack, *The German Army on the Somme 1914–1916*
(Pen & Sword Books, Barnsley, 2005)

Strong, Paul, and Marble, Sanders, *Artillery in the Great War*
(Pen & Sword Books, Barnsley, 2011)

In addition, a range of regimental histories was consulted, from those of the regiments disbanded in 1922 and written by officers who had served in the First World War to more recent studies, some of which, such as *At War with the 16th Irish Division 1914–1918: The Staniforth Letters*, are based on primary documents, in this instance the letters of John (Max) Staniforth of 7th Leinsters (later 2nd Leinsters), edited by Richard Grayson.

Richard Doherty

Writer, historian and broadcaster Richard Doherty has twenty-eight books on military and police history to his credit; two were nominated for the prestigious Templer Medal. As well as researching, writing and presenting several historical series for BBC Radio Ulster, he has presented two major historical programmes for BBC TV, and contributed to, or advised on, many programmes for Radio Ulster, Radio Four, RTE and independent producers. His Radio Ulster programme on the North African campaign, in the *Sons of Ulster* series, was nominated for a Sony Award. He has addressed audiences in the UK, Republic of Ireland, France and Italy, as well as the United States, where he has lectured at the US Marine Corps Staff and Command College. In addition to leading battlefield studies and tours in Ireland, Normandy, Italy and Greece, he writes historical articles, book reviews and commentaries for newspapers, magazines and journals, is Chairman of the Irish Regiments Historical Society, a member of military history societies in the UK, Ireland and the USA, a trustee of two regimental museums and of the International School for Peace Studies, as well as being a trustee and member of the Council of the Northern Ireland War Memorial.